Tucholsky Wagner Zola Scott Sydow Freud Schlegel
Turgenev Wallace Fonatne Twain Walther von der Vogelweide Fouqué Friedrich II. von Preußen
Weber Freiligrath Kant Ernst Frey
Fechner Fichte Weiße Rose von Fallersleben Richthofen Frommel
Engels Fielding Hölderlin
Fehrs Faber Flaubert Eichendorff Tacitus Dumas
Eliasberg Ebner Eschenbach
Feuerbach Maximilian I. von Habsburg Fock Zweig
Eliot Vergil
Ewald London
Goethe Elisabeth von Österreich
Mendelssohn Balzac Shakespeare Dostojewski Ganghofer
Lichtenberg Rathenau Doyle Gjellerup
Trackl Stevenson Hambruch
Mommsen Tolstoi Lenz Hanrieder Droste-Hülshoff
Thoma von Arnim Hägele Hauff Humboldt
Dach Verne
Reuter Rousseau Hagen Hauptmann Gautier
Karrillon Garschin
Defoe Hebbel Baudelaire
Damaschke Descartes
Hegel Kussmaul Herder
Wolfram von Eschenbach Dickens Schopenhauer Rilke George
Bronner Darwin Melville Grimm Jerome
Campe Horváth Aristoteles Bebel Proust
Bismarck Vigny Barlach Voltaire Federer Herodot
Gengenbach Heine
Storm Casanova Tersteegen Grillparzer Georgy
Chamberlain Lessing Langbein Gilm Gryphius
Brentano Lafontaine
Strachwitz Claudius Schiller Kralik Iffland Sokrates
Bellamy Schilling
Katharina II. von Rußland Gerstäcker Raabe Gibbon Tschechow
Löns Hesse Hoffmann Gogol Wilde Gleim Vulpius
Luther Heym Hofmannsthal Klee Hölty Morgenstern Goedicke
Roth Heyse Klopstock Kleist
Luxemburg Puschkin Homer Mörike Musil
Machiavelli La Roche Horaz
Navarra Aurel Musset Kierkegaard Kraft Kraus
Nestroy Marie de France Lamprecht Kind Kirchhoff Hugo Moltke
Laotse Ipsen Liebknecht
Nietzsche Nansen Ringelnatz
Marx Lassalle Gorki Klett Leibniz
von Ossietzky May vom Stein Lawrence Irving
Petalozzi Knigge
Platon Pückler Michelangelo Kafka
Sachs Poe Kock
de Sade Praetorius Mistral Liebermann Korolenko
Zetkin

The publishing house tredition has created the series **TREDITION CLASSICS**. It contains classical literature works from over two thousand years. Most of these titles have been out of print and off the bookstore shelves for decades.

The book series is intended to preserve the cultural legacy and to promote the timeless works of classical literature. As a reader of a **TREDITION CLASSICS** book, the reader supports the mission to save many of the amazing works of world literature from oblivion.

The symbol of **TREDITION CLASSICS** is Johannes Gutenberg (1400 – 1468), the inventor of movable type printing.

With the series, tredition intends to make thousands of international literature classics available in printed format again – worldwide.

All books are available at book retailers worldwide in paperback and in hardcover. For more information please visit: www.tredition.com

tredition was established in 2006 by Sandra Latusseck and Soenke Schulz. Based in Hamburg, Germany, tredition offers publishing solutions to authors and publishing houses, combined with worldwide distribution of printed and digital book content. tredition is uniquely positioned to enable authors and publishing houses to create books on their own terms and without conventional manufacturing risks.

For more information please visit: www.tredition.com

Discovery of Muscovy

Richard Hakluyt

Imprint

This book is part of the TREDITION CLASSICS series.

Author: Richard Hakluyt
Cover design: toepferschumann, Berlin (Germany)

Publisher: tredition GmbH, Hamburg (Germany)
ISBN: 978-3-8491-4974-1

www.tredition.com
www.tredition.de

THE DISCOVERY OF MUSCOVY ETC.

Contents:

INTRODUCTION

The first relations between England and Russia were established in Queen Elizabeth's reign, in the manner here set forth, by the expedition undertaken by Sir Hugh Willoughby and completed by Richard Chanceler or Chancellor, captain of the Edward Bonaventure. Chanceler went on after Willoughby and the crew of his ship, The Admiral, with the crew of another vessel in the expedition, had been parted from Chanceler in a storm in the North Sea, and Willoughby's men were all frozen to death. A few men belonging to the other ship were believed to have found their way back to England. The story of Chanceler's voyage and the following endeavours to open Muscovy to English trade is here given, as it was told in Hakluyt's collection of "The Principal Navigations, Voyages, and Discoveries made by the English Nation," the folio published in 1589.

The story of our first contact with Russia belongs to the days of Ivan the Terrible. The Russians are a Slavonic people, with Finnish elements to the North and Mongolian to the South, and old contact with the Swedes, from whom they are supposed to have got their name through the Finnish Ruotsi, a corruption, it is said, of the Swedish rothsmenn—rowers. Legends point also to a Scandinavian settlement in the ninth century in Northern Russia. A chief Igor, whose name is supposed to represent the Scandinavian Ingvar, was trained by a warrior chief Oleg (Scandinavian Helgi?), who attacked Byzantium and wrung tribute from the Greeks. After the death of Oleg, Igor reigned, and after the death of Igor his wife Olga was regent, and was baptised at Byzantium in the year 955. Her son Sviotoslaff the first chief with a Slavonic name, was a conquering chief, who did not become Christian. He was killed in battle, and his skull was made into a drinking-cup. His son Vladimir was a cruel warrior, who took to Christianity, was baptised in the year 988, and caused the image of the Slavonic god of Thunder, Perun, to be first cudgelled and then thrown into a river. Vladimir, who first introduced Christianity, divided his dominions, leaving Novgorod to his son Yaroslaff, who established the first code of laws. After the death of Yaroslaff, in the year 1054, Russia was broken into petty principalities, until the year 1238, when there was a great invasion of the Mongols, who became a great disturbing power, and remained so until the year 1462, when Ivan III. began the consolidation of a Russian empire. He reigned forty-three years, suppressed the liberties of many independent regions, annexed states, checked the Mongols, married a Byzantine princess, and so brought Greek culture into Moscow. Ivan III. bequeathed his throne to a son Basil, who made further addition to the dominions of Muscovy, and treated with foreign princes. Herberstein, an ambassador to him from Germany, has left a description of his court. Then followed the reign of Basil's son Ivan IV., Ivan the Terrible, who was, when his father died, a child of three years old. He was at first, from 1533 to 1538, under the care of his mother, Helen Glinska, a Pole. In 1543, when a boy of thirteen, he broke loose from the tutelage of chiefs, and caused one of them who had most worried him to be torn to pieces by dogs. In 1547, at the age of seventeen, he was crowned, and took the title of Czar (Caesar). He married a good wife, submitted to the guidance of a good priest, Silvester, revised his grandfather's code of laws, issued a code for the Church, conquered enemies upon his borders, had desires towards the civilisation of the West, and did nothing to earn his name of "the Terrible" before the year 1558, five years after the setting out of Willoughby and Chancellor. His cruelties continued from 1558 until his death, in 1584.

H. M.

THE NEW NAVIGATION AND DISCOVERY OF THE KINGDOM OF MUSCOVY
By the North-East in the year 1553: Enterprised by SIR HUGH WILLOUGHBIE, KNIGHT, performed by RICHARD CHANCELER, Pilot-major of
the voyage. Translated out of the Latin into English.

At what time our merchants perceived the commodities and wares of England to be in small request with the countries and people about us, and near unto us, and that those merchandises which strangers in the time and memory of our ancestors did earnestly seek and desire were now neglected, and the price thereof abated, although by us carried to their own ports, and all foreign merchandises in great account, and their prices wonderfully raised; certain grave citizens of London, and men of great wisdom, and careful of the good of their country, began to think with themselves how this mischief might be remedied: neither was a remedy (as it then appeared) wanting to their desires for the avoiding of so great an inconvenience: for seeing that the wealth of the Spaniards and Portuguese, by the discovery and search of new trades and countries, was marvellously increased, supposing the same to be a course and means for them also to obtain the like, they thereupon resolved upon a new and strange navigation. And whereas at the same time one Sebastian Cabot, a man in those days very renowned, happened to be in London, they began first of all to deal and consult diligently with him, and after much speech and conference together, it was at last concluded that three ships should be prepared and furnished out for the search and discovery of the Northern part of the world, to open a way and passage to our men for travel to new and unknown kingdoms.

And whereas many things seemed necessary to be regarded in this so hard and difficult a matter, they first made choice of certain grave and wise persons in manner of a senate or company which should lay their heads together and give their judgments and provide things requisite and profitable for all occasions; by this company it was thought expedient that a certain sum of money should publicly be collected to serve for the furnishing of so many ships. And lest any private man should be too much oppressed and charged, a course was taken that every man willing to be of the society should disburse the portion of twenty and five pounds apiece, so that in a short time by this means the sum of six thousand pounds being gathered, the three ships were bought, the most part whereof they provided to be newly built and trimmed. But in this action, I wot not whether I may more admire the care of the merchants, or the diligence of the shipwrights: for the merchants, they get very strong and well seasoned planks for the building, the shipwrights, they with daily travail and their greatest skill, do fit them for the dispatch of the ships, they caulk them, pitch them, and among the rest, they make one most staunch and firm, by an excellent and ingenious invention. For they had heard that in certain parts of the ocean a kind of worm is bred which many times pierceth and eateth through the strongest oak that is, and therefore that the mariners and the rest to be employed in this voyage might be free and safe from this danger, they cover a piece of the keel of the ship with thin sheets of lead; and having thus built the ships, and furnished them with armour and artillery, then followed a second care no less troublesome and necessary than the former, namely the provision of victuals which was to be made according to the time and length of the voyage. And whereas they afore determined to have the east part of the world sailed unto, and yet that the sea towards the same was not open, except they kept the northern tract where as yet it was doubtful whether there were any passage yea or no, they resolved to victual the ships for eighteen months, which they did for this reason. For our men being to pass that huge and cold part of the world, they wisely foreseeing it, allow them six months' victual to sail to the place, so much more to remain there if the extremity of the winter hindered their return, and so much more also for the time of their coming home.

Now this provision being made and carried aboard, with armour and munition of all sorts, sufficient captains and governors of so great an enterprise were as yet wanting: to which office and place, although many men (and some void of experience) offered themselves, yet one Sir Hugh Willoughbie, a most valiant gentleman, and well born, very earnestly requested to have that care and charge committed unto him: of whom before all others, both by reason of his goodly personage (for he was of a tall stature) as also for his singular skill in the services of war, the Company of the merchants made greatest account: so that at the last they concluded and made choice of him for the general of this voyage, and appointed to him the admiral, with authority and command over all the rest. And for the government of the other ships although divers men seemed willing, and made offers of themselves thereunto, yet by a common consent one Richard Chanceler, a man of great estimation for many good parts of wit in him, was elected, in whom alone great hope for the performance of this business rested. This man was brought up by one Master Henry Sidney, a noble young gentleman and very much beloved of King Edward, who this time coming to the place where the merchants were gathered together, began a very eloquent speech or oration, and spake to them after this manner following:-

"My very worshipful friends, I cannot but greatly commend your present godly and virtuous intention in the serious enterprising (for the singular love you bear to your country), a matter which (I hope) will prove profitable for this nation, and honourable to this our land. Which intention of yours we also of the nobility are ready to our power to help and further: neither do we hold anything so dear and precious unto us, which we will not willingly forego, and lay out in so commendable a cause. But principally I rejoice in myself, that I have nourished and maintained that wit which is like by some means and in some measure to profit and stead you in this worthy action. But yet I would not have you ignorant of this one thing, that I do now part with Chanceler not because I make little reckoning of the man, or that his maintenance is burdensome and chargeable unto me, but that you might conceive and understand my goodwill and promptitude for the furtherance of this business, and that the authority and estimation which he deserveth may be given him. You know the man by report, I by experience, you by words, I by deeds, you by speech and company, but I by the daily trial of his life, have a full and perfect knowledge of him. And you are also to remember into how many perils for your sakes, and his country's love, he is now to run: whereof it is requisite that we be not un-mindful, if it please God to send him good success. We commit a little money to the chance and hazard of fortune: he commits his life (a thing to a man of all things most dear) to the raging sea, and the uncertainties of many dangers. We shall here live and rest at home, quietly with our friends and acquaintance; but he in the meantime labouring to keep the ignorant and unruly mariners in good order and obedience, with how many cares shall he trouble and bear him-self, with how many troubles shall he break himself, and how many disquietings shall he be forced to sustain: we shall keep our own coasts and country, he shall seek strange and unknown kingdoms. He shall commit his safety to barbarous and cruel people, and shall hazard his life amongst the monstrous and terrible beasts of the sea. Wherefore in respect of the greatness of the dangers, and the excellency of his charge, you are to favour and love the man thus departing from us, and if it falls so happily out that he return again, it is your part and duty also liberally to reward him."

After that this noble young gentleman had delivered this or some such like speech, much more eloquently than I can possibly report it, the company then present began one to look upon another, one to question and confer with one another; and some (to whom the virtue and sufficiency of the man was known) began secretly to rejoice with themselves and to conceive a special hope, that the man would prove in time very rare and excellent, and that his virtues already appearing and shining to the world would grow to the great honour and advancement of this kingdom.

After all this, the company growing to some silence, it seemed good to them that were of greatest gravity amongst them to inquire, search, and seek what might be learned and known concerning the easterly part or tract of the world. For which cause two Tartars (Tartarians) which were then of the king's stable were sent for, and an interpreter was gotten to be present, by whom they were demanded touching their country, and the manners of their nation. But they were able to answer nothing to the purpose: being indeed more acquainted (as one there merrily and openly said) to toss pots than to learn the states and dispositions of people. But after much ado and many things passed about this matter, they grew at last to this issue, to set down and appoint a time for the departure of the ships: because divers were of opinion that a great part of the best time of the year was already spent, and if the delay grew longer the way would be stopped and hard by the frost of the ice, and the cold climate; and therefore it was thought best by the opinion of them all that by the 20th day of May the captains and mariners should take shipping and depart from Ratcliffe upon the ebb, if it so pleased God. They having saluted their acquaintance, one his wife, another his children, another his kinsfolks, and another his friends dearer than his kinsfolks, were present and ready at the day appointed, and having weighed anchor, they departed with the turning of the water, and sailing easily, came first to Greenwich. The greater ships were towed down with boats and oars, and the mariners being all apparelled in watchet or sky-coloured cloth, rowed amain, and made way with diligence. And being come near to Greenwich (where the court then lay), presently upon the news thereof the courtiers came running out, and the common people flocked together, standing very thick upon the shore: the Privy Council they looked out at the windows of the court, and the rest ran by to the tops of the towers: the ships hereupon discharge their ordnance and shoot off their pieces after the manner of war and of the sea, insomuch that the tops of the hills sounded therewith, the valleys and the waters gave an echo, and the mariners they shouted in such sort that the sky rang again with the noise thereof. One stood in the poop of the ship, and by his gesture bids farewell to his friends in the best manner he could. Another walks upon the hatches, another climbs the shrouds, another stands upon the main yard, and another in the top of the ship. To be short, it was a very triumph (after a sort) in all respects to the beholders. But, alas, the good King Edward (in respect of whom principally all this was prepared) he only by reason of his sickness was absent from this show, and not long after the departure of these ships, the lamentable and most sorrowful accident of his death followed.

But to proceed in the matter. The ships going down with the tide, came at last to Woolwich where they stayed and cast anchor, with purpose to depart therehence again, as soon as the turning of the water and a better wind should draw them to set sail. After this they departed and came to Harwich, in which port they stayed long, not without great loss and consuming of time; yet at the last with a good wind they hoisted up sail, and committed themselves to the sea, giving their last adieu to their native country, which they knew not whether they should ever return to see again or not. Many of them looked oftentimes back, and could not refrain from tears, considering into what hazards they were to fall, and what uncertainties of the sea they were to make trial of.

Amongst the rest Richard Chanceler, the captain of the Edward Bonaventure, was not a little grieved with the fear of wanting victuals, part whereof was found to be corrupt and putrified at Harwich, and the hogsheads of wine also leaked, and were not staunch; his natural and fatherly affection also somewhat troubled him, for he left behind him his two little sons, which were in the case of orphans if he sped not well; the estate also of his company moved him to care, being in the former respects after a sort unhappy, and were to abide with himself every good or bad accident; but in the meantime while his mind was thus tormented with the multiplicity of sorrows and cares, after many days' sailing they kenned land afar off whereunto the pilots directed the ships; and being come to it they land, and find it to be Rose Island, where they stayed certain days, and afterwards set sail again, and, proceeding towards the north, they espied certain other islands which were called the Cross of Islands. From which places when they were a little departed Master Willoughbie the General, a man of good foresight and providence in all his actions, erected and set out his flag, by which he called together the chiefest men of the other ships, that by the help and assistance of their councils the order of the government and conduction of the ships in the whole voyage might be the better: who being come together accordingly, they conclude and agree that if any great tempest should arise at any time, and happen to disperse and scatter them, every ship should endeavour his best to go to Wardhouse, a haven or castle of some name in the kingdom of Norway, and that they that arrived there first in safety should stay and expect the coming of the rest.

The very same day in the afternoon, about four of the clock, so great a tempest suddenly arose, and the seas were so outrageous, that the ships could not keep their intended course, but some were perforce driven one way and some another way, to their great peril and hazard. The General, with his loudest voice, cried out to Richard Chanceler and earnestly requested him not to go far from him; but he neither would nor could keep company with him if he sailed still so fast, for the Admiral was of better sail than his ship. But the said Admiral (I know not by what means), bearing all his sails, was carried away with so great force and swiftness, that not long after he was quite out of sight, and the third ship also, with the same storm and like rage, was dispersed and lost us.

The ship-boat of the Admiral, striking against the ship, was overwhelmed in the sight and view of the mariners of the Bonaventure; and as for them that are already returned and arrived, they know nothing of the rest of the ships what was become of them.

But if it be so that any miserable mishap have overtaken them, if the rage and fury of the sea have devoured those good men, or if as yet they live, and wander up and down in strange countries, I must needs say they were men worthy of better fortune; and if they be living, let us wish them safety and a good return, but if the cruelty of death hath taken hold of them, God send them a Christian grave and sepulchre.

Now, Richard Chanceler with his ship and company being thus left alone, and become very pensive, heavy, and sorrowful by this dispersion of the fleet, he (according to the order before taken) shapeth his course for Wardhouse, in Norway, there to expect and abide the arrival of the rest of the ships. And being come thither, and having stayed there the space of seven days, and looked in vain for their coming, he determined at length to proceed alone in the purposed voyage; and as he was preparing himself to the part, it happened that he fell in company and speech with certain Scottish men, who having understanding of his intention, and wishing well to his actions, began earnestly to dissuade him from the further prosecution of the discovery by amplifying the dangers which he was to fall into, and omitted no reason that might serve to that purpose.

But he holding nothing so ignominious and reproachful as inconstancy and levity of mind, and persuading himself that a man of valour could not commit a more dishonourable part than for fear of danger to avoid and shun great attempts, was nothing at all changed or discouraged with the speeches and words of the Scots, remaining steadfast and immutable in his first resolution; determining either to bring that to pass which was intended or else to die the death.

And as for them which were with Master Chanceler in his ship, although they had great cause of discomfort by the loss of their company (whom the aforesaid tempest had separated from them), and were not a little troubled with cogitations and perturbations of mind in respect of their doubtful course, yet, notwithstanding, they were of such content and agreement of mind with Master Chanceler, that they were resolute and prepared under his direction and government to make proof and trial of all adventures without all fear or mistrust of future dangers. Which constancy of mind in all the company did exceedingly increase their captain's carefulness; for he being swallowed up with like goodwill and love towards them, feared lest, through any error of his, the safety of the company should be endangered. To conclude, when they saw their desire and hope of the arrival of the rest of the ships to be every day more and more frustrated, they provided to sea again, and Master Chanceler held on his course towards that unknown part of the world, and sailed so far that he came at last to the place where he found no night at all, but a continual light and brightness of the sun shining clearly upon the huge and mighty sea. And having the benefit of this perpetual light for certain days, at length it pleased God to bring them into a certain great bay, which was of one hundred miles or thereabout over. Whereinto they entered and somewhat far within it cast anchor, and looking every way about them, it happened that they espied afar off a certain fisher boat, which Master Chanceler, accompanied with a few of his men, went towards to commune with the fishermen that were in it, and to know of them what country it was, and what people, and of what manner of living they were. But they being amazed with the strange greatness of his ship (for in those parts before that time they had never seen the like), began presently to avoid and to flee. But he still following them, at last overtook them, and being come to them, they (being in great fear as men half dead) prostrated themselves before him, offering to kiss his feet; but he (according to his great and singular courtesy) looked pleasantly upon them, comforting them by signs and gestures, refusing those duties and reverences of theirs, and taking them up in all loving sort from the ground. And it is strange to consider how much they were afterwards in that place this humanity of his did purchase to himself. For they being dismissed, spread byand-by a report abroad of the arrival of a strange nation of a singular gentleness and courtesy, whereupon the common people came together offering to those new-come guests victuals freely, and not refusing to traffic with them, except they had been bound by a certain religious use and custom not to buy any foreign commodities without the knowledge and consent of the king.

By this time our men had learned that this country was called Russia or Muscovy, and that Ivan Vasilivich (which was at that time their king's name) ruled and governed far and wide in those places. And the barbarous Russians asked likewise of our men whence they were and what they came for. Whereunto answer was made that they were Englishmen sent into those coasts from the most excellent King Edward VI., having from him in commandment certain things to deliver to their king, and seeking nothing else but his amity and friendship and traffic with his people, whereby they doubted not but that great commodity and profit would grow to the subjects of both kingdoms. The barbarians heard these things very gladly, and promised their aid and furtherance to acquaint their king out of hand with so honest and reasonable a request.

In the meantime Master Chanceler entreated victuals for his money of the governor of that place, who, together with others, came aboard him, and required hostages of them likewise for the more assurance of safety to himself and his company. To whom the governors answered that they knew not in that case the will of their king, and yet were willing in such things as they might lawfully do to pleasure him, which was as then to afford him the benefit of victuals. Now whilst these things were a-doing, they secretly sent a messenger unto the Emperor to certify him of the arrival of a strange nation, and withal to know his pleasure concerning them. Which message was very welcome unto him, insomuch that voluntarily he invited them to come to his court. But if by reason of the tediousness of so long a journey they thought it not best so to do, then he granted liberty to his subjects to bargain and to traffic with them. And further promised that if it would please them to come to him, he himself would bear the whole charges of post-horses. In the meantime the governors of the place deferred the matter from day to day, pretending divers excuses, and saying one while that the consent of all the governors, and another while that the great and weighty affairs of the kingdom compelled them to defer their answer. And this they did of purpose, so long to protract the time until the messenger (sent before to the king) did return with relation of his will and pleasure.

But Master Chanceler (seeing himself held in this suspense with long and vain expectation and thinking that of intention to delude him, they posted the matter off so often) was very instant with them to perform their promise, which if they would not do he told them that he would depart and proceed in his voyage. So that the Muscovites (although as yet they knew not the mind of their king) yet fearing the departure indeed of our men, who had such wares and commodities as they greatly desired, they at last resolved to furnish our people with all things necessary, and to conduct them by land to the presence of their king. And so Master Chanceler began his journey, which was very long and most troublesome, wherein he had the use of certain sledges which in that country are very common, for they are carried themselves upon sledges, and all their carriages are in the same sort, the people almost not knowing any other manner of carriage, the cause whereof is the exceeding hardness of the ground, congealed in the winter time by the force of the cold, which in those places is very extreme and horrible, whereof hereafter we will say something. But now, they having passed the greater part of their journey, met at last with the sledgeman (of whom I spake before) sent to the king secretly from the justices or governors, who by some ill-hap had lost his way, and had gone to the seaside which is near to the country of the Tartars, thinking there to have found our ship. But having long erred and wandered out of his way, at the last in his direct return, he met, as he was coming, our Captain on the way. To whom he by-and-by delivered the Emperor's letters, which were written to him with all courtesy, and in the most loving manner that could be: wherein express commandment was given that post horses should be gotten for him and the rest of his company without any money. Which thing was of all the Russians in the rest of their journey so willingly done, that they began to quarrel, yea, and to fight also in striving and contending which of them should put their post-horses to the sled: so that after much ado, and great pains taken in this long and weary journey (for they had travelled very near fifteen hundred miles), Master Chanceler came at last to Moscow, the chief city of the kingdom, and the seat of the king, of which city, and of the Emperor himself, and of the principal cities of Muscovy, we will speak immediately more at large in this discourse.

OF MUSCOVY, WHICH IS ALSO CALLED RUSSIA

Muscovy, which hath the name also of Russia the White, is a very large and spacious country, every way bounded with divers nations. Towards the south and east it is compassed with Tartaria, the northern side of it stretcheth to the Scythian Ocean; upon the west part border the Lappians, a rude and savage nation, living in woods, whose language is not known to any other people; next unto these, more towards the south, is Swecia, then Finlandia, then Livonia, and last of all Lithuania. This country of Muscovy hath also very many and great rivers in it, and is marsh ground in many places; and as for the rivers, the greatest and most famous amongst all the rest is that which the Russians in their own tongue call Volga, but others know it by the name of Rha. Next unto it in fame is Tanais, which they call Don, and the third Boristhenes, which at this day they call Dnieper. Two of these — to wit, Rha and Boristhenes — issuing both out of one fountain, run very far through the land: Rha receiving many other pleasant rivers into it, and running from the very head or spring of it towards the east, after many crooked turnings and windings, dischargeth itself and all the other waters and rivers that fall into it, by divers passages into the Caspian Sea. Tanais, springing from a fountain of great name in those parts, growing great near to his head, spreads itself at length very largely and makes a great lake; and then growing narrow again, doth so run for certain miles until it fall into another lake, which they call Ivan: and there hence, fetching a very crooked course, comes very near to the river Volga; but disdaining, as it were, the company of any other river, doth there turn itself again from Volga, and runs towards the south, and falls at last into the Lake of Moeotis. Boristhenes, which comes from the same head that Rha doth (as we said before), carrieth both itself, and other waters that are near unto it, towards the south, not refusing the mixture of other small rivers; and, running by many great and large countries, falls at last into Pontus Euxinus. Besides these rivers are also in Muscovy certain lakes and pools — the lakes breed fish by the celestial influence, and amongst them all the chiefest and most principal is called Belij Jesera, which is very famous by reason of a very strong tower built in it, wherein the kings of Muscovy reserve and repose their treasure in all time of war and danger.

Touching the Riphean Mountains, whereupon the snow lieth continually, and where hence in times past it was thought that Tanais the river did spring, and that the rest of the wonders of Nature which the Grecians feigned and invented of old were there to be seen, our men which lately came from thence neither saw them, nor yet have brought home any perfect relation of them, although they remained there for the space of three months, and had gotten in that time some intelligence of the language of Muscovy. The whole country is plain and champaign, and few hills in it; and towards the north it hath very large and spacious woods, wherein is great store of fir-trees — a wood very necessary and fit for the building of houses. There are also wild beasts bred in those woods, as buffes, bears, and black wolves, and another kind of beast unknown to us, but called by them "roffomakka;" and the nature of the same is very rare and wonderful, for when it is great with young, and ready to bring forth, it seeketh out some narrow place between two stakes, and so going through them, presseth itself, and by that means is eased of her burden, which otherwise could not be done. They hunt their buffes for the most part a-horseback, but their bears afoot, with wooden forks. The north parts of the country are reported to be so cold, that the very ice or water which distilleth out of the moist wood which they lay upon the fire is presently congealed and frozen, the diversity growing suddenly to be so great, that in one and the selfsame firebrand a man shall see both fire and ice. When the winter doth once begin there it doth still more and more increase by a perpetuity of cold; neither doth that cold slake until the force of the sunbeams doth dissolve the cold and make glad the earth, returning to it again. Our mariners which we left in the ship in the meantime to keep it, in their going up only from their cabins to the hatches, had their breath oftentimes so suddenly taken away, that they eftsoons fell down as men very near dead, so great is the sharpness of that cold climate; but as for the south parts of the country, they are somewhat more temperate.

OF MOSCOW, THE CHIEF CITY OF THE KINGDOM, AND OF THE EMPEROR THEREOF.

It remaineth that a large discourse be made of Moscow, the principal city of that country, and of the prince also, as before we have promised. The empire and government of the king is very large, and his wealth at this time exceeding great. And because the city of Moscow is the chiefest of all the rest, it seemeth of itself to challenge the first place in this discourse. Our men say, that in bigness it is as great as the city of London, with the suburbs thereof. There are many and great buildings in it, but, for beauty and fairness, nothing comparable to ours. There are many towns and villages also, but built out of order and with no handsomeness; their streets and ways are not paved with stone as ours are; the walls of their houses are of wood; the roofs, for the most part, are covered with shingle boards. There is hard by the city a very fair castle, strong, and furnished with artillery, whereunto the city is joined directly towards the north with a brick wall; the walls also of the castle are built with brick, and are in breadth or thickness eighteen feet. This castle hath on the one side a dry ditch, and on the other side the river Volga, whereby it is made almost impregnable. The same Volga, trending towards the east, doth admit into it the company of the River Occa.

In the castle aforesaid there are in number nine churches or chapels, not altogether unhandsome, which are used and kept by certain religious men, over whom there is, after a sort, a patriarch or governor, and with him other reverend fathers, all which for the greater part dwell within the castle. As for the king's court and palace, it is not of the neatest, only in form it is four-square and of low building, much surpassed and excelled by the beauty and elegancy of the houses of the kings of England. The windows are very narrowly built, and some of them by glass, some other by lattices admit the light; and whereas the palaces of our princes are decked and adorned with hangings of cloth of gold, there is none such there; they build and join to all their walls benches, and that not only in the court of the emperor, but in all private men's houses.

Now after that they had remained about twelve days in the city, there was then a messenger sent unto them to bring them to the king's house, and they being after a sort wearied with their long stay, were very ready and willing so to do; and, being entered within the gates of the court, there sat a very honourable company of courtiers, to the number of one hundred, all apparelled in cloth of gold down to their ankles, and therehence being conducted into the chamber of presence, our men began to wonder at the majesty of the Emperor. His seat was aloft in a very royal throne, having on his head a diadem or crown of gold, apparelled with a robe all of goldsmith's work, and in his hand he held a sceptre garnished and beset with precious stones; and, besides all other notes and appearances of honour, there was a majesty in his countenance proportionable with the excellency of his estate. On the one side of him stood his Chief Secretary, and on the other side the Great Commander of Silence, both of them arrayed also in cloth of gold; and then there sat the Council, of one hundred and fifty in number, all in like sort arrayed, and of great state. This so honourable an assembly, so great a majesty of the Emperor and of the place, might very well have amazed our men, and have dashed them out of countenance; but, notwithstanding, Master Chanceler, being therewithal nothing dismayed, saluted and did his duty to the Emperor after the manner of England, and withal delivered unto him the letters of their King Edward VI. The Emperor having taken and read the letters, began a little to question with them, and to ask them of the welfare of our king, whereunto our men answered him directly and in few words. Hereupon our men presented something to the Emperor by the Chief Secretary, which at the delivery of it put off his hat, being before all the time covered; and so the Emperor having invited them to dinner, dismissed them from his presence; and going into the chamber of him that was Master of the Requests to the Emperor, and having stayed there the space of two hours, at the last the messenger cometh, and calleth them to dinner. They go, and being conducted into the Golden Court (for so they call it, although not very fair), they find the Emperor sitting upon a high and stately seat, apparelled with a robe of silver, and with another diadem on his head; our men, being placed over against him, sit down. In the midst of the room stood a mighty cupboard upon a square foot, whereupon stood also a round board, in manner of a diamond, broad beneath, and towards the top narrow, and every step rose up more narrow than the other. Upon this cupboard was placed the

Emperor's plate, which was so much that the very cupboard itself was scant able to sustain the weight of it. The better part of all the vessels and goblets was made of very fine gold; and, amongst the rest, there were four pots of very large bigness, which did adorn the rest of the plate in great measure, for they were so high, that they thought them at the least five feet long. There were also upon this cupboard certain silver casks, not much differing from the quantity of our firkins, wherein was reserved the Emperor's drink. On each side of the hall stood four tables, each of them laid and covered with very clean table-cloths, whereunto the company ascended by three steps or degrees, all which were filled with the assembly present. The guests were all apparelled with linen without, and with rich skins within, and so did notably set out this royal feast. The Emperor, when he takes any bread or knife into his hand, doth first of all cross himself upon his forehead. They that are in special favour with the Emperor sit upon the same bench with him, but somewhat far from him; and before the coming in of the meat the Emperor himself, according to an ancient custom of the Kings of Muscovy, doth first bestow a piece of bread upon every one of his guests, with a loud pronunciation of his title and honour in this manner, "The Great Duke of Muscovy and Chief Emperor of Russia, John Basiliwich (and then the officer nameth the guest), doth give thee bread," whereupon all the guests rise up and by-and-by sit down again. This done, the Gentleman Usher of the hall comes in with a notable company of servants carrying the dishes, and having done his reverence to the Emperor, puts a young swan in a golden platter upon the table, and immediately takes it thence again, delivering it to the carver and seven other of his fellows to be cut up, which being performed, the meat is then distributed to the guests with the like pomp and ceremonies. In the meantime, the Gentleman Usher receives his bread and talketh to the Emperor, and afterward, having done his reverence, he departeth. Touching the rest of the dishes, because they were brought in out of order, our men can report no certainty; but this is true, that all the furniture of dishes and drinking vessels, which were then for the use of a hundred guests, was all of pure gold, and the tables were so laden with vessels of gold, that there was no room for some to stand upon them.

We may not forget that there were one hundred and forty servitors arrayed in cloth of gold, that in the dinner-time changed thrice their habit and apparel, which servitors are in like sort served with bread from the Emperor as the rest of the guests. Last of all, dinner being ended, and candles brought in (for by this time night was come), the Emperor calleth all his guests and noblemen by their names, in such sort that it seems miraculous that a prince, otherwise occupied in great matters of estate, should so well remember so many and sundry particular names. The Russians told our men that the reason thereof, as also of the bestowing of bread in like manner, was to the end that the Emperor might keep the knowledge of his own household, and withal, that such as are under his displeasure might by this means be known.

OF THE DISCIPLINE OF WAR AMONGST THE RUSSIANS.

Whensoever the injuries of their neighbours do call the king forth to battle, he never armeth a less number against the enemy than three hundred thousand soldiers, one hundred thousand whereof he carrieth into the field with him, and leaveth the rest in garrison in some fit places for the better safety of his empire. He presseth no husbandmen nor merchant; for the country is so populous that these being left at home the youth of the realm is sufficient for all his wars. As many as go out to warfare do provide all things of their own cost; they fight not on foot, but altogether on horseback: their armour is a coat of mail, and a helmet; the coat of mail without is gilded, or else adorned with silk, although it pertain to a common soldier; they have a great pride in showing their wealth; they use bows and arrows as the Turks do; they carry lances also into the field. They ride with a short stirrup after the manner of the Turks; they are a kind of people most sparing in diet, and most patient in extremity of cold above all others. For when the ground is covered with snow, and is grown terrible and hard with the frost, this Russian hangs up his mantle or soldier's coat against that part from whence the wind and snow drives, and so making a little fire, lieth down with his back towards the weather; this mantle of his serves him for his bed, wall, house and all; his drink is the cold water of the river, mingled with oatmeal, and this is all his good cheer, and he thinketh himself well and daintily fed therewith, and so sitteth down by his fire, and upon the hard ground, roasteth, as it were, his weary sides thus daintily stuffed; the hard ground is his feather bed, and some block or stone his pillow; and as for his horse, he is, as it were, a chamber-fellow with his master, faring both alike. How justly may this barbarous and rude Russian condemn the daintiness and niceness of our captains, who, living in a soil and air much more temperate, yet commonly use fur boots and cloaks! but thus much of the furniture of their common soldiers. But those that are of higher degrees come into the field a little better provided. As for the furniture of the Emperor himself, it is then above all other times most notable. The coverings of his tent for the most part are all of gold, adorned with stones of great price, and with the curious workmanship of plumasiers; as often as they are to skirmish with the enemy, they go forth without any order at all; they make no wings, nor military divisions of their men, as we do, but lying for the most part in ambush, do suddenly set upon the enemy. Their horses can well abstain two whole days from any meat. They feed upon the barks of trees and the most tender branches in all the time of war. And this scant and miserable manner of living both the horse and his master can well endure, sometimes for the space of two months lusty and in good state of body. If any man behave himself valiantly in the field to the contentation of the Emperor, he bestoweth upon him in recompense of his service some farm or so much ground as he and his may live upon, which, notwithstanding, after his death returneth again to the Emperor if he die without a male issue. For although his daughters be never so many, yet no part of that inheritance comes to them, except, peradventure, the Emperor of his goodness give some portion of the land amongst them to bestow them withal. As for the man, whosoever he be, that is in this sort rewarded by the Emperor's liberality, he is bound in a great sum to maintain so many soldiers for the war, when need shall require, as that land in the opinion of the Emperor is able to maintain. And all those to whom any land falls by inheritance are in no better condition, for if they die without any male issue, all their lands fall into the hands of the Emperor; as, moreover, if there be any rich man amongst them, who in his own person is unfit for the wars, and yet hath such wealth, that thereby many noblemen and warriors might be maintained, if any of the courtries present his name to the Emperor, the unhappy man is by- and-by sent for, and in that instant deprived of all his riches, which with great pains and travail all his lifetime he had gotten together, except perhaps some small portion thereof be left him to maintain his wife, children, and family. But all this is done of all people so willingly at the Emperor's commandment, that a man would think they would rather make restitution of other men's goods than give that which is their own to other men. Now the Emperor having taken these goods into his hands, bestoweth them among his courtiers according to their deserts, and the oftener that a man is sent to the wars, the more favour he thinketh is borne to him by the Emperor, although he go upon his own charge, as I said before. So great is the obedience of all men generally to their prince.

OF THE AMBASSADORS OF THE EMPEROR OF MUSCOVY.

The Muscovite, with no less pomp and magnificence than that which we have spoken of, sends his ambassadors to foreign princes in the affairs of estate. For while our men were abiding in the city of Moscow, there were two ambassadors sent to the King of Poland, accompanied with 500 notable horse; and the greater part of the men were arrayed in cloth of gold and of silk, and the worst apparel was of garments of a blue colour, to speak nothing of the trappings of the horses, which were adorned with gold and silver, and very curiously embroidered; they had also with them one hundred white and fair spare horses, to use them at such times as any weariness came upon them. But now the time requireth me to speak briefly of other cities of the Muscovites, and of the wares and commodities that the country yieldeth.

NOVOGORODE.

Next unto Moscow, the city of Novogorode is reputed the chiefest of Russia; for although it be in majesty inferior to it, yet in greatness it goeth beyond it. It is the chiefest and greatest mart town of all Muscovy; and albeit the Emperor's seat is not there, but at Moscow, yet the commodiousness of the river falling into the gulf which is called Sinus Finnicus, whereby it is well frequented by merchants, makes it more famous than Moscow itself. This town excels all the rest in the commodities of flax and hemp; it yields also hides, honey, and wax. The Flemings there sometimes had a house of merchandise, but by reason that they used the like ill- dealing there which they did with us they lost their privileges—a restitution whereof they earnestly sued for at the time that our men were there. But those Flemings, hearing of the arrival of our men in those parts, wrote their letters to the Emperor against them, accusing them for pirates and rovers, wishing them to detain and imprison them; which things, when they were known of our men, they conceived fear that they should never have returned home. But the Emperor, believing rather the king's letters which our men brought than the lying and false suggestions of the Flemings, used no ill treaty towards them.

YERASLAVE.

Yeraslave also is a town of some good fame for the commodities of hides, tallow, and corn, which it yields in great abundance. Cakes of wax are there also to be sold, although other places have greater store; this Yeraslave is distant from Moscow about two hundred miles, and betwixt them are many populous villages. Their fields yield such store of corn, that in conveying it towards Moscow, sometimes in a forenoon, a man shall see seven hundred or eight hundred sleds going and coming, laden with corn and salt fish; the people come a thousand miles to Moscow to buy that corn, and then carry it away upon sleds; and these are those people that dwell in the north parts, where the cold is so terrible that no corn doth grow there, or, if it spring up, it never comes to ripeness. The commodities that they bring with them are salt fish, skins, and hides.

VOLOGDA.

Vologda being from Moscow five hundred and fifty miles, yields the commodities of hemp and flax, although the greatest store of flax is sold at Novogorode.

PLESCO.

The town of Plesco is frequented of merchants for the good store of honey and wax that it yieldeth.

COLMAGRO.

The north parts of Russia yield very rare and precious skins; and amongst the rest those principally which we call sables, worn about the necks of our noblewomen and ladies. It hath also martens' skins, white, black, and red fox skins, skins of hares and ermines and others, which they call and term barbarously as beavers, minxes, and minevers. The sea adjoining breeds a certain beast which they call mors, which seeketh his food upon the rocks, climbing up with the help of his teeth. The Russians used to take them for the great virtue that is in their teeth, whereof they make as great account as we do of the elephant's tooth. These commodities they carry upon deers' backs to the town of Lampas; and from thence to Colmagro, and there in the winter time are kept great fairs for the sale of them. This city of Colmagro serves all the country about with salt and salt fish. The Russians also of the north parts send thither oil which they call train, which they make in a river called "Vna," although it be also made elsewhere; and here they used to boil the water of the sea, whereof they make very great store of salt.

OF CONTROVERSIES IN LAW, AND HOW THEY ARE ENDED.

Having hitherto spoken so much of the chiefest cities of Russia as the matter required, it remaineth that we speak somewhat of the laws that the Muscovites do use, as far forth as the same are come to our knowledge. If any controversy arise among them they first make their landlords judges in the matter, and if they cannot end it, then they prefer it to the magistrate. The plaintiff craveth of the said magistrate that he may have leave to enter law against his adversary, and having obtained it, the officer fetcheth the defendant and beateth him on the legs till he bring forth a surety for him; and if he be not of such credit as to procure a surety, then are his hands by an officer tied to his neck, and he is beaten all the way till he come before the judge. The judge then asketh him (as, for example, in the matter of debt) whether he oweth anything to the plaintiff. If he denies it, then saith the judge, "How canst thou deny it?" The defendant answereth by an oath; thereupon the officer is commanded to cease from beating of him until the matter be further tried. They have no lawyers, but every man is his own advocate; and both the complaint of the accuser and the answer of the defendant are in manner of petition delivered to the Emperor, entreating justice at his hands. The Emperor himself heareth every great controversy, and, upon the hearing of it, giveth judgment, and that with great equity, which I take to be a thing worthy of special commendation in the majesty of a prince. But although he do this with a good purpose of mind, yet the corrupt magistrates do wonderfully pervert the same; but if the Emperor take them in any fault, he doth punish them most severely. Now at the last, when each party hath defended his cause with his best reasons, the judge demandeth of the accuser whether he hath any more to say for himself. He answereth that he will try the matter in fight by his champion, or else entreateth that in fight betwixt themselves the matter may be ended, which being granted, they both fight it out; or if both of them, or either of them, seem unfit for that kind of trial, then they have public champions to be hired which live by ending of quarrels. These champions are armed with iron axes and spears, and fight on foot; and he whose champion is overcome is by- and-by taken and imprisoned and terribly handled, until he agree with his adversary. But if either of them be of any good calling and degree, and do challenge one another to fight, the judge granteth it; in which case they may not use public champions. And he that is of any good birth doth contemn the other if he be basely born, and will not fight with him. If a poor man happen to grow in debt, his creditor takes him, and maketh him pay the debt in working either to himself or to some other man whose wages he taketh up. And there are some among them that used willingly to make themselves, their wives, and children bondslaves unto rich men — to have a little money at the first into their hands, and so for ever after content themselves with meat and drink, so little account do they make of liberty.

OF PUNISHMENTS UPON THIEVES.

If any man be taken upon committing of theft, he is imprisoned, and often beaten, but not hanged for the first offence, as the manner is with us; and this they call the law of mercy. He that offendeth the second time hath his nose cut off, and is burnt in the forehead with a hot iron. The third time he is hanged. There are many cut-purses among them, and if the rigour of the prince did not cut them off, they could not be avoided.

OF THEIR RELIGION.

They maintain the opinions of the Greek Church; they suffer no graven images of saints in their churches, but their pictures painted in tables they have in great abundance, which they do adore, and offer unto and burn wax candles before them, and cast holy water upon them, without other honour. They say that our images, which are set up in churches, and carved, have no divinity in them. In their private houses they have images for their household saints, and, for the most part, they are put in the darkest place of the house; he that comes into his neighbour's house doth first salute his saints, although he see them not. If any form or stool stand in his way, he oftentimes beateth his brow upon the same, and often, ducking down with his head and body, worshippeth the chief image. The habit and attire of the priests and of the laymen doth nothing at all differ; as for marriage, it is forbidden to no man: only this is received, and held amongst them for a rule and custom, that if a priest's wife do die, he may not marry again nor take a second wife; and, therefore, they of secular priests, as they call them, are made monks, to whom then chastity for ever is commanded. Their divine service is all done and said in their own language, that every man may understand it; they receive the Lord's Supper with leavened bread, and after the consecration they carry it about the church in a saucer, and prohibit no man from receiving and taking of it that is willing so to do. They use both the Old and the New Testament, and read both in their own language, but so confusedly that they themselves that do read understand not what they themselves do say; and while any part of either Testament is read there is liberty given by custom to prattle, talk, and make a noise; but in the time of the rest of the service they use very great silence and reverence, and behave themselves very modestly and in good sort. As touching the Lord's Prayer, the tenth man amongst them knows it not; and for the Articles of our Faith and the Ten Commandments, no man, or, at the least, very few of them, do either know them or can say them: their opinion is that such secret and holy things as they are should not rashly and imprudently be communicated with the common people. They hold for a maxim amongst them that the old Law, and the Commandments also, are all abolished by the death and blood of Christ; all studies and letters of humanity they utterly refuse; concerning the Latin, Greek, and Hebrew tongues, they are altogether ignorant in them.

Every year they celebrate four several fasts, which they call according to the names of the saints: the first begins with them at the time that our Lent begins; the second is called amongst them the

Fast of St. Peter; the third is taken from the Day of the Virgin Mary; and the fourth, and last, begins upon St. Philip's Day. But as we begin our Lent upon Wednesday, so they begin theirs upon the Sunday. Upon the Saturday they eat flesh. Whensoever any of those fasting feasts do draw near, look what week doth immediately go before them; the same week they live altogether upon white meats, and in their common language they call those weeks the fast of butter.

In the time of their fasts the neighbours everywhere go from one to another, and visit one another, and kiss one another with kisses of peace, in token of their mutual love and Christian concord; and then also they do more often than at any other time go to the Holy Communion. When seven days are past, from the beginning of the fast, then they often do either go to their churches or keep themselves at home and use often prayer; and for that seven nights they eat nothing but herbs; but after that seven night fast is once past, then they return to their old intemperance of drinking, for they are notable toss-pots. As for the keeping of their fasting days, they do it very straitly, neither do they eat anything besides herbs and salt fish as long as those fasting days do endure; but upon every Wednesday and Friday, in every week throughout the year, they fast.

There are very many monasteries of the order of Saint Benedict amongst them, to which many great livings, for their maintenance, do belong; for the friars and the monks do at the least possess the third part of the livings throughout the whole Muscovite Empire. To those monks that are of this order there is amongst them a perpetual prohibition that they may eat no flesh; and, therefore, their meat is only salt fish, milk, and butter; neither is it permitted them by the laws and customs of their religion to eat any fresh fish at all, and at those four fasting times whereof we spake before they eat no fish at all: only they live with herbs, and cucumbers, which they do continually for that purpose cause, and take order, to grow and spring for their use and diet.

As for their drink, it is very weak and small. For the discharge of their office they do every day say service, and that early in the mornings, before day; and they do in such sort and with such observation begin their service, that they will be sure to make an end of it before day; and about nine of the clock in the morning they celebrate the Communion. When they have so done they go to dinner, and after dinner they go again to service, and the like also after supper; and in the meantime, while they are at dinner, there is some exposition or interpretation of the Gospel used.

Whensoever any abbot of any monastery dieth, the Emperor taketh all his household stuff, beasts, flocks of sheep, gold, silver, and all that he hath, or else he that is to succeed him in his place and dignity doth redeem all those things, and buyeth them of the Emperor for money.

Their churches are built of timber, and the towers of their churches for the most part are covered with shingle boards. At the doors of their churches they usually build some entrance or porch, as we do, and in their churchyards they erect a certain house of wood, wherein they set up their bells—wherein sometimes they have but one, in some two, and in some also three.

There is one use and custom amongst them which is strange and rare, yet it is very ridiculous, and that is this: when any man dieth amongst them they take the dead body and put it in a coffin or chest, and in the hand of the corpse they put a little scroll, and in the same there are these words written, that the same man died a Russian of Russia, having received the faith and died in the same. This writing or letter they say they send to St. Peter, who, receiving it (as they affirm), reads it, and by-and-by admits him into heaven, and that his glory and place is higher and greater than the glory of the Christians of the Latin Church, reputing themselves to be followers of a more sincere faith and religion than they; they hold opinion that we are but half Christians, and themselves only to be the true and perfect Church—these are the foolish and childish dotages of such ignorant barbarians.

ON THE MUSCOVITES THAT ARE IDOLATERS, DWELLING NEAR TO TARTARIA.

There is a certain part of Muscovy, bordering upon the countries of the Tartars, wherein those Muscovites that dwell are very great idolaters; they have one famous idol amongst them, which they call the Golden Old Wife, and they have a custom that whensoever any plague or any calamity doth afflict the country, as hunger, war, or such like, then they go by-and-by to consult with their idol, which they do after this manner: they fall down prostrate before the idol, and pray unto it, and put in the presence of the same a cymbal, and about the same certain persons stand, which are chosen amongst them by lot: upon their cymbal they place a silver toad, and sound the cymbal, and to whomsoever of those lotted persons that toad goeth he is taken, and by-and-by slain; and immediately, I know not by what illusions of the devil or idol, he is again restored to life, and then doth reveal and deliver the causes of the present calamity. And by this means knowing how to pacify the idol, they are delivered from the imminent danger.

OF THE FORM OF THEIR PRIVATE HOUSES, AND OF THE APPAREL OF THE PEOPLE.

The common houses of the country are everywhere built of beams of fir-trees; the lower beams do so receive the round hollowness of the uppermost, that by the means of the building thereupon they resist and expel all winds that blow, and where the timber is joined together, there they stop the chinks with moss. The form and fashion of their houses in all places is four-square, with straight and narrow windows, whereby with a transparent easement made or covered with skin like to parchment they receive the light. The roofs of their houses are made of boards covered without with the bark of trees: within their houses they have benches or grieves hard by their walls, which commonly they sleep upon, for the common people know not the use of beds: they have stoves wherein in the morning they make a fire, and the same fire doth either moderately warm or make very hot the whole house.

The apparel of the people for the most part is made of wool, their caps are picked like unto a rike or diamond, broad beneath, and sharp upward. In the manner of making whereof there is a sign and representation of nobility; for the loftier or higher their caps are, the greater is their birth supposed to be, and the greater reverence is given them by the common people.

THE CONCLUSION TO QUEEN MARY.

These are the things, most excellent Queen, which your subjects newly returned from Russia have brought home concerning the state of that country: wherefore if your Majesty shall be favourable, and grant a continuance of the travel, there is no doubt but that the honour and renown of your name will be spread amongst those nations, whereunto three only noble personages from the very creation have had access, to whom no man hath been comparable.

THE COPY OF THE DUKE OF MUSCOVY AND EMPEROR OR RUSSIA HIS LETTERS, SENT TO KING EDWARD VI., BY THE HANDS OF RICHARD CHANCELER.

"The almighty power of God, and the incomprehensible Holy Trinity, rightful Christian belief, etc. We, great Duke Ivan Vasilivich, by the grace of God Emperor of all Russia, and great Duke of Vladermerskij, Moskowskij, Novogrodskij, Cazanskii, Pskanskii, Smolenskii, Tuerskij, Hugorskij, Permskii, Veatskii, Bolgarskii, with divers other lands, Emperor also and great Duke of Novogoroda, and in the low countries of Chernigouskii, Rezanskii, Volotskii, Refskii, Belskii, Rostouskii, Yaroslavskii; Belocherskii, Oodorskii, Obdorskii, Codinskii, and many other countries, lord over all the north coast, greeting.

"Before all right great and worthy of honour Edward, King of England, &c., according to our most hearty and good zeal, with good intent and friendly desire, and according to our holy Christian Faith and great governance, and being in the light of great understanding, our answer by this our honourable writing unto your kingly governance, at the request of your faithful servant Richard Chanceler, with his company, as they shall let you wisely know, is thus. In the strength of the twentieth year of our governance, be it known, that at our sea coasts arrived a ship, with one Richard and his company, and said, that he was desirous to come into our dominions, and according to his request hath seen our Majesty and our eyes; and hath declared unto us your Majesty's desire as that we should grant unto your subjects, to go and come, and in our dominions, and among our subjects to frequent free marts, with all sorts of merchandises, and upon the same to have wares for their return. And they have also delivered us your letters which declare the same request. And hereupon we have given order, that wheresoever your faithful servant Hugh Willoughbie land or touch in our dominions, to be well entertained, who as yet is not arrived, as your servant Richard can declare.

"And we, with Christian belief and faithfulness, and according to your honourable request and my honourable commandment will not leave it undone, and are furthermore willing that you send unto us your ships and vessels, when, and as often as they may have passage, with good assurance on our part to see them harmless. And if you send one of your Majesty's council to treat with us, whereby your country merchants may with all kinds of wares, and where they will, make their market in our dominions, they shall have their free mart with all free liberties through my whole dominions with all kinds of wares, to come and go at their pleasure, without any let, damage, or impediment, according to this our letter, our word, and our seal, which we have commanded to be under-sealed. Written in our dominion in our town and in our palace in the Castle of Moscow, in the year seven thousand and sixty, the second month of February."

This letter was written in the Muscovian tongue, in letters much like to the Greek letters, very fair written on paper with a broad seal hanging at the same, sealed in paper upon wax. This seal was much like the broad seal of England, having on the one side the image of a man on horseback in complete harness fighting with a dragon.

Under this letter was another paper written in the Dutch tongue, which was the interpretation of the other written in the Muscovian letters. These letters were sent the next year after the date of King Edward's letters, 1554.

THE COINS, WEIGHTS, AND MEASURES, USED IN RUSSIA
Written by JOHN HASSE in the year 1554.

Forasmuch as it is most necessary for all merchants which seek to have traffic in any strange regions, first to acquaint themselves with the coins of those lands with which they do intend to join in traffic, and how they are called from the valuation of the highest piece to the lowest, and in what sort they make their payments, as also what their common weights and measures be. For these causes I have thought good to write something thereof, according to mine own knowledge and experience, to the end that the merchants of that new adventure may the better understand how the wealth of that new frequented trade will arise.

First, it is to be noted that the Emperor of Russia hath no other coins than silver in all his land which goeth for payment amongst merchants; yet, notwithstanding, there is a coin of copper, which serveth for the relief of the poor in Moscow, and nowhere else, and that is but only for quas, water, and fruit—as nuts, apples, and such like. The name of which money is called pole or poles, of which poles there go to the least of the silver coins eighteen. But I will not stand upon this, because it is no current money amongst merchants.

Of silver coins there be these sorts of pieces: the least is a poledenga; the second, a denga; the third, nowgrote, which is as much to say in English, as halfpenny, penny, and twopence; and for other valued money than this there is none. There are oftentimes there coins of gold, but they come out of foreign countries; whereof there is no ordinary valuation, but they pass according to the agreement of merchants.

Their order in summing of money is this: as we say in England, halfpenny, penny, shilling, and pound, so say they, poledenga, denga, altine, and rubble (rouble). There goeth two poledengas to a denga, six dengaes to an altine, and twenty-three altines and two dengaes to a rubble.

Concerning the weights of Russia, they are these. There are two sorts of pounds in use amongst them — the one great, the other small. The great pound is just two small pounds; they call the great weight by the name of beasemar, and the small they call the skalla-waight. With this small weight they weigh their silver coins, of which the Emperor hath commanded to put to every small pound three rubbles of silver; and with the same weight they weigh all grocery wares, and almost all other wares, which come into the land, except those which they weigh by the pode, as hops, salt, iron, lead, tin, and batrie, with divers others. Notwithstanding, they used to weigh batrie more often by the small weight than by the great.

Whensoever you find the prices of your wares rated by the pode, consider that to be the great weight, and the pound to be small. Also they divide the small pound into forty-eight parts, and they call the eight-and-fortieth part a slotnike, by the which slotnike the retailers sell their wares out of their shops, as goldsmiths, grocers, silk-sellers, and such other, like as we do use to retail by the ounce. And as for their great weight, which they call the beasemar, they sell by pode or ship pound. The pode doth contain of the great weight, forty pounds; and of the small, eighty. There go ten podes to a ship pound.

Yet you must consider that their great weight is not full with ours; for I take not their great pound to be full thirteen ounces, but above twelve I think it be. But for your just proof, weigh six rubbles of Russian money with our pound weight, and then shall you see what it lacketh; for six rubbles of Russia is, by the Emperor's stand-ard, the great pound. So that I think it the next way to know the just weight as well of the great pound as of the small.

There is another weight needful to be known, which is the weight of Wardhouse; for so much as they weigh all their dry fish by weight, which weight is the basemere as they of Russia do use, notwithstanding there is another sort in it. The names of those weights are these: the marke pound, the great pound, the wee and the ship pound. The marke pound is to be understood as our pound, and their great is twenty-four of their marke pound; the wee is three great pound; and eight wee is a ship pound.

Now, concerning their measures. As they have two sorts of weights, so they have also two sorts of measures, wherewith they measure cloth, both linen and woollen. They call the one an areshine, and the other a locut. The areshine I take to be as much as the Flanders ell, and their locut half an English yard. With their areshine they may mete all such sorts of cloths as cometh into the land, and with the locut all such cloth, both linen and woollen, as they make themselves. And whereas we used to give yard and inch, or yard and handfull, they do give nothing but bare measure.

They have also a measure wherewith they do mete their corn, which they call a set-forth, and the half of that an osmine. This set-forth I take to be three bushels of London measure. And as for their drink measure, they call it a spanne, which is much like a bucket; and of that I never saw any true rate, but that some was greater than other some. And as for the measures of Wardhouse, wherewith they mete their cloth, there is no difference between that and the measure of danske, which in half an English ell.

Concerning the tolls and customs of Russia, it was reported to me in Muscovy that the Turks and Armenians pay the tenth penny custom of all the wares they bring into the Emperor's land, and above that they pay for all such goods as they weigh at the Emperor's beam two pence of the rouble, which the buyer or seller must make report of to the master of the beam. They also pay a certain horse toll, which is in divers places of his realm four pence of a horse.

The Dutch nation are free of this; notwithstanding for certain offences, they had lost their privileges, which they have recovered this summer, to their great charge. It was reported to me by a justice of that country, that they paid for it thirty thousand roubles, and also that Rye, Dorpt, and Revel, have yielded themselves under the government of the Emperor of Russia; whether this was a brag of the Russians or not, I know not, but thus he said, and, indeed, while we were there, there came a great ambassador out of Liffeland for the assurance of their privileges.

To speak somewhat of the commodities of this country, it is to be understood that there is a certain place fourscore miles from the sea called Colmogro; to which place there resort all the sorts of wares that are in the north parts — as oils, salt, stock-fish, salmon, feathers, and furs; their salt they make of salt water by the seaside; their oils they make of seals, whereof they have great store, which is brought out of the bay where our ships came in; they make it in the spring of the year, and bring it to Colmogro to sell, and the merchants there carry it to Novogrod, and so sell it to the Dutch nation. Their stock-fish and salmon cometh from a place called Mallums, not far from Wardhouse; their salmon and their salt they carry to Moscow, and their dried fish they carry to Novogrod, and sell it there to the Leeflanders.

The furs and feathers which come to Colmogro, as sables, beavers, minks, ermine lettis, graies, wolverins, and white foxes, with deer- skins, they are brought thither by the men of Penninge, Lampne, and Powstezer, which fetch them from the Samoydes that are counted savage people, and the merchants that bring these furs do use to truck with the merchants of Colmogro for cloth, tin, batrie, and such other like, and the merchants of Colmogro, carry them to Novogrod, Vologda, or Moscow, and sell them there. The feathers which come from Penning they do little esteem.

If our merchants do desire to know the meetest place of Russia for their standing house; in mine opinion I take it to be Vologda, which is a great town standing in the heart of Russia with many great and good towns about it. There is great plenty of corn, victuals, and of all such wares as are raised in Russland (Russia), but specially flax, hemp, tallow, and bacon; there is also great store of wax, but it cometh from Moscow.

The town of Vologda is meetest for our merchants, because it lieth amongst all the best towns of Russia, and there is no town in Russia but trades with it; also the water is a great commodity to it. If they plant themselves in Moscow or Novogrod their charge will be great and wonderful, but not so in Vologda, for all things will there be had better cheap by the one-half; and for their vent, I know no place so meet; it is likely that some will think the Moscow to be the meetest by the reason of the court, but by that reason I take it to be worse; for the charge there would be so great by cravers and expenses that the moiety of the profit would be wholly consumed, which in the other place will be saved. And yet, notwithstanding, our merchants may be there in the winter to serve the Emperor and his Court. The Emperor is a great merchant himself of wax and sables, which with good foresight may be procured to their hands; as for other commodities there are little or none in Muscovy besides those above rehearsed; if there be other it is brought thither by the Turks, who will be dainty to buy our cloths considering the charges of carriages overland.

Our merchants may do well to provide for the Russians such wares as the Dutch nation doth serve them of, as Flanders and Holland cloths, which I believe they shall serve better with less charge than they of Rye or Dorpt, or Revel; for it is no small adventure to bring their cloths out of Flanders to either of these places, and their charge not little to carry them overland to Novogrod which is from Rye nine hundred Russian miles.

This Novogrod is a place well furnished with flax, wax, hides, tallow, and many other things; the best flax in Russia is brought thither, and there sold by the hundred bundles, which is done also at Vologda, and they that bring the flax to Novogrod dwell as near Vologda as Novogrod, and when they hear of the utterance which they may have with our nation, they will as willingly come to them as go to the other.

They have in Russia two sorts of flax, the one is called great flax, and the other small; that which they call great flax is better by four roubles in a hundred bundles than the small. It is much longer than the other, and cleaner, without wood; and whereas of the small flax there go twenty-seven or twenty-eight bundles to a ship pound; there goeth not of the greater sort above twenty-two or twenty-four at the most. There are many other trifles in Russia, as soap, mats, &c., but I think there will be no great account made of them.

Articles conceived and determined for the Commission of the Merchants of this Company resiant (resident) in Russia, and at the Wardhouse, for the second voyage, 1555, the first of May, as followeth.

First the governor, consuls, assistants, and whole company assembled this day in open Court committeth and authoriseth Richard Gray and George Killingworth jointly and severally to be agents, factors, and attorneys, general and special, for the whole body of this company; to buy, sell, truck, change, and permute, all and every kind and kinds of wares, merchandises, and goods, to the said company appertaining, now laden and shipped in the good ship called the Edward Bonaventure, appointed for Russia, the same to utter and sell to the most commodity, profit, and advantage of the said corporation, be it for ready money, wares, and merchandises, or truck, presently, or for time, as occasion and benefit of the company shall require, and all such wares as they or either of them shall buy, truck, or provide, or cause to be bought for the company to lade them homeward in good order and condition, as by prudent course of merchandises shall, and ought to appertain, which article extendeth also to John Brooke for the Wardhouse, as in the seventeenth and eighteenth articles of this commission appeareth.

2. Item, it is also committed, as above, to the said agents, to bind and charge the said company by debt for wares upon credit, as good opportunity and occasion shall serve, with power to charge and bind the said company and their successors for the payments of such things as shall be taken up for credit, and the said agents to be relieved, ab opere satis dandi.

3. Item, full authority and power is committed to the said first-named factors, together with Richard Chanceler, grand pilot of this fleet, to repair to the Emperor's court, there to present the King and Queen's Majesty's letters, written in Greek, Polish, and Italian, and to give and exhibit the merchants' presents at such time and place as shall be thought most expedient; they, or one of them, to demand, and humbly desire of the Emperor, such further grants and privileges to be made to this company as may be beneficial for the same,

to continue in traffic with his subjects, according to such instructions as be in this behalf devised and delivered to the agents whereunto relation is to be had, and some one of these persons to attend upon the court for the obtaining of the same, as to their discretions shall be thought good.

4. Item, that all the said agents do well consider, ponder, and weigh such articles as be delivered to them, to know the natures, dispositions, laws, customs, manners, and behaviours of the people of the countries where they shall traffic, as well of the nobility as of the lawyers, merchants, mariners, and common people, and to note diligently the subtleties of their bargaining, buying and selling, making as few debts as possibly may be; and to be circumspect, that no law, neither of religion nor positive, be broken or transgressed by them, or any minister under them, nor yet by any mariner or other person of our nation; and to foresee that all tolls, customs, and such other rights, be so duly paid, that no forfeiture or confiscation may ensue to our goods either outward or inward; and that all things pass with quiet, without breach of the public peace or common tranquillity of any of the places where they shall arrive or traffic.

5. Item, that provision be made in Moscow or elsewhere, in one or more good towns, where good trade shall be found for a house or houses for the agents and company to inhabit and dwell at your accustomed diets, with warehouses, cellars, and other houses of offices requisite; and that none of the inferior ministers, of what place or vocation soever he be, do lie out of the house of the agents without license to be given; and that every inferior officer shall be obedient to the orders, rules, and governments of the said agents; and in case any disobedient person shall be found among any of them, then such person to be punished for his misbehaviour at the discretion of the said agents, or of one of them in the absence of the other.

6. Item, if any person of the said ministers shall be of such pride or obstinacy, that after one or two honest admonitions he will not be reformed nor reconciled from his faults, then the said agents to displace every such person from the place or room to him here

committed, and some other discreet person to occupy the same, as to the said agents by their discretions shall seem meet.

7. Item, if any person shall be found so arrogant, that he will not be ordered nor reformed by the said agents, or by one of them in the absence of the other, then the said person to be delivered to the justice of the country, to receive such punishment as the laws of the country do require.

8. Item, that the said agents and factors shall daily one hour in the morning confer and consult together what shall be most convenient and beneficial for the company; and such orders as they shall determine, to be written by the secretary of the company, in a book to be provided for that purpose; and no inferior person to infringe or break any such order or device, but to observe the same exactly, upon such reasonable pain as the agents shall put him to by discretion.

9. Item, that the said agents shall in the end of every week, or oftener, as occasion shall require, peruse, see, and try, not only the cashier's books, reckonings, and accounts, firming the same with their hands, but also shall receive and take weekly the account of every other officer, as well of the vendes, as of the empteous, and also of the state of the household expenses, making thereof a perfect declaration as shall appertain; the same accounts also to be firmed by the said agents' hands.

10. Item, that no inferior minister shall take upon him to make any bargain or sale of any wares, merchandises, or goods, but by the commission and warranties of the said agents under their hands; and he not to transgress his commission by any way, pretence, or colour.

11. Item, that every inferior minister—that is to understand, all clerks and young merchants being at the order of the said agents— shall ride, go, sail, and travel to all such place and places as they or he shall be, appointed unto by the said agents, and effectually to follow and do that which to him or them shall be committed, well and truly to the most benefit of the company, according to the charge to him or them committed, even as by their oaths, duties, and bonds of their masters they be bounden and charged to do.

12. Item, that at every month's end all accounts and reckonings shall be brought into perfect order into the ledger or memorial; and the decrees, orders, and rules of the agents, together with the privileges and copies of letters, may and shall be well and truly written by the secretary, in such form as shall be appointed for it, and that the copies of all their doings may be sent home with the said ship at her return.

13. Item, that all the agents do diligently learn and observe all kinds of wares, as well naturals as foreign, that be beneficial for this realm, to be sold for the benefit of the company; and what kind of our commodities and other things of these west parts be most vendable in those realms with profit, giving a perfect advice of all such things requisite.

14. Item, if the Emperor will enter into bargain with you for the whole mass of your stock, and will have the trade of it to utter to his own subjects, then debating the matter prudently among yourselves, set such high prices of your commodities as you may assure yourselves to be gainers in your own wares, and yet — to buy theirs at such base prices as you may here also make a commodity and gain at home, having in your minds the notable charges that the company have defrayed in advancing this voyage; and the great charges that they sustain daily in wages, victuals, and other things, all which must be requited by the wise handling of this voyage, which, being the first precedent shall be a perpetual precedent for ever; and therefore all circumspection is to be used; and foreseeing in this first enterprise, which God bless and prosper under you to His glory and the public wealth of this realm, whereof the Queen's majesty and the Lords of the Council have conceived great hope, whose expectations are not to be frustrated.

15. Item, it is to be had in mind that you use all ways and means possible to learn how men may pass from Russia, either by land or by sea, to Cathaia, and what may be heard of our other ships, and to what knowledge you may come, by conferring with the learned or well- travelled persons, either natural or foreign, such as have travelled from the north to the south.

16. Item, it is committed to the said agents that, if they shall be certified credibly that any of our said first ships be arrived in any

place whereunto passage is to be had by water or by land, that then certain of the company, at the discretion of the agents, shall be appointed to be sent to them to learn their estate and condition, to visit, refresh, relieve, and furnish them with all necessaries and requisites at the common charges of the company, and to embrace, accept, and entreat them as our dear and well-beloved brethren of this our society to their rejoicing and comfort, advertising Sir Hugh Willoughbie and others of our carefulness of them and their long absence, with our desire to hear of them, with all other things done in their absence for their commodity, no less than if they had been present.

17. Item, it is decreed that, when the ships shall arrive at this going forth at the Wardhouse, that their agents—with Master Chanceler, grand pilot; John Brooke, merchant, deputed for the Wardhouse, with John Backhand, master of the Edward; John Howlet, master, and John Robbins, pilot, of the Philip and Mary—shall confer and consult together that is most profitable to be done therefore for the benefit of the company, and to consider whether they may bargain with the captain of the Castle, and the inhabitants in that place, or along the coast for a large quantity of fish—dry or wet— killed by the naturals, or to be taken by our men at a price reasonable for truck of cloth, meal, salt, or beer, and what train- oil or other commodity is to be had there at this time, or any other season of the year; and whether there will be had or found sufficient lading for both the said ships to be bought there, and how they may confer with the naturals for a continuance in haunting the place, if profit will so arise to the company; and to consider whether the Edward in her return may receive at the Wardhouse any kind of lading homeward, and what it may amount unto, and whether it shall be expedient for the Philip to abide at Wardhouse the return of the Edward out of Russia, or getting that she may return with the first good wind to England without abiding for the Edward; and so to conclude and accord certainly among themselves upon their arrival that the certainty may (upon good deliberation) be so ordered and determined between both ships that the one may be assured of the other; and their determinations to be put in writing duplicate to remain with each ship, according to such order as shall be taken between them.

18. Item, that John Brooke, our merchant for the Wardhouse, take good advice of the rest of our agents how to use himself in all affairs while the ship shall be at the Wardhouse; he to see good order to be kept, and make bargains advisedly, not crediting the people until their natures, dispositions, and fidelities shall be well tried; make no debts, but to take ware for ware in hand, and rather be trusted than to trust. Note diligently what be the best wares for those parts, and how the fish falleth on the coast, and by what means it is to be bought at the most advantage, what kinds and diversities of sorts in fishes be, and whether it will keep better in bulk piled or in cask.

19. Item, he to have a diligent eye and circumspection to the beer, salt, and other liquid wares, and not to suffer any waste to be made by the company; and he in all contracts to require advice, counsel, and consent of the master and pilot; the merchant to be our house-wife, as our special trust is in him. He to tender that no laws nor customs of the country be broken by any of the company, and to render to the prince and other officers all that which to them doth appertain—the company to be quiet, void of all quarrelling, fighting, or vexation; abstain from all excess of drinking as much as may be, and in all to use and behave themselves as to quiet merchants doth and ought to appertain.

20. Item, it is decreed by the company that the Edward shall return home this year with as much wares as may be conveniently and profitably provided, bought and laden in Russia, and the rest to be taken in at the Wardhouse as by the agents shall be accorded. But by all means it is to be foreseen and noted that the Edward return home, and not to winter in any foreign place, but to come home, and bring with her all the whole advertisements of the merchants, with such further advices for the next year's provisions as they shall give.

21. Item, it is further decreed and ordained inviolably to be observed, that when the good ships, or either of them (by God's grace) shall return home to the coast of England, that neither of them shall stay or touch in any haven or port of England, otherwise than wind and weather shall serve, but shall directly sail and come to the port of the city of London, the place of their right discharge; and that no bulk be broken, hatches open, chest, fardell, truss, barrell, fat, or

whatsoever thing it shall be, be brought out of the ship, until the company shall give order for the same, and appoint such persons of the company as shall be thought meet for that purpose, to take view and consider the ship and her lading, and shall give order for the breaking up of the said bulk, or give license by discretion, for things to be brought to land. And that every officer shall show the invoice of his charge to him first committed, and to examine the wastes and losses, and to deliver the remainder to the use and benefit of the company, according to such order as shall be appointed in that behalf.

22. Item, the company exhorteth, willeth, requireth, not only all the said agents, pilots, masters, merchants, clerks, boatswains, stewards, skafemasters, and all other officers and ministers of this present voyage, being put in charge and trust daily to peruse, read, and study, such instructions as be made, given, and delivered to them for perfect knowledge of the people of Russia, Muscovy, Wardhouse, and other places; their dispositions, laws, manners, customs, uses, tolls, carriages, coins, weights, numbers, measures, wares, merchandises, commodities and incommodities, the one to be accepted and embraced, the other to be rejected and utterly abandoned, to the intent that every man taking charge, may be so well taught, perfected, and readily instructed, in all the premises, that, by ignorance, no loss or prejudice may grow or chance to the company, assuring themselves, that forasmuch as the company hath travailed and laboured so in these their instructions to them given, that every man may be perfect, and fully learned to eschew all losses, hurts, and damages, that may ensue by pretence or colour of none knowledge, the company extendeth not to allow, or accept ignorance for any lawful or just cause of excuse, in that which shall be misordered by negligence, the burthen whereof shall light upon the negligent offending person, especially upon such as of their own heads, or temerity, will take upon him or them to do or to attempt anything, whereby prejudice may arise, without the commission of the agents as above is mentioned, whereunto relation be had.

23. Forasmuch as it is not possible to write and indite such prescribed orders, rules, and commissions to you the agents and factors, but that occasion, time, and place, and the pleasures of the princes, together with the operation or success of fortune, shall

change or shift the same, although not in the whole, yet in part, therefore the said company do commit to you their dear and entire beloved agents and factors, to do in this behalf for the commodity and wealth of this company, as by your discretions, upon good advised deliberations, shall be thought good and beneficial. Provided always that the honour, good-name, fame, credit, and estimation of the same company be conserved and preserved; which to confirm we beseech the living Lord to his glory, the public benefit of this realm, our common profit, and your praises.

Finally, for the service and due accomplishment of all the premises, every agent and minister of, and for, this voyage hath not only given a corporal oath upon the Evangelists to observe, and cause to be observed, this commission, and every part, clause, and sentence of the same, as much as in him lieth, as well for his own part as for any other person, but also have bound themselves and their friends to the company in several sums of money, expressed in the acts and records of this society, for the truth and fidelities of them for the better, and also manifester testification of the truth, and of their oaths, promises, and bands aforesaid, they have to this commission subscribed particularly their several hands, and the company also in confirmation of the same, have set their seal. Given the day, month, and years first above mentioned.

THE OATH MINISTERED TO THE SERVANTS OF THE FELLOWSHIP.

Ye swear by the holy contents of that book, that ye shall well, faithfully, and truly and uprightly, and with all your endeavour, serve this right worshipful company in that order, which by this fellowship's agent or agents in the dominions of the Emperor of Russia, &c., shall be unto you committed, by commission, commandment, or other his direction. And that you shall be obedient and faithful to the same, our agent or agents, and that well and truly and uprightly, according to the commission, charge, commandment, or other direction of the said agent or agents to you from time to time given and to be given, you shall prosecute and do all that which in you lieth for the good renown, commodity, benefit, and profit of the said fellowship; and you shall not, directly or indirectly, openly or covertly, do, exercise, or use any hide or feat of merchandises for your own private account, commodity, gain, or profit, or for the account of or for any other person or persons without consent or license of this said fellowship first obtained in writing. And if you shall know or understand any other person or persons to use, exercise, or do any trade, traffic, or feat of merchandise to or for his or their own account or accounts, at any time or times hereafter, that then ye shall truly and plainly disclose, open, utter, and reveal, and show the same unto the said fellowship, without fraud, colour, covin, or delay: So help you God, &c.

THE LETTER OF MASTER GEORGE KILLINGWORTH, THE COMPANY'S FIRST AGENT
IN MUSCOVY,
Touching their entertainment in their second voyage. Anno 1555, the
27th of November, in Moscow.

Right worshipful, my duty considered, &c. — It may please your worship to understand that at the making hereof we all be in good health, thanks be to God, save only William, our cook, as we came from Colmogro fell into the river out of the boat and was drowned. And the 11th day of September we came to Vologda, and there we laid all our wares up, and sold very little; but one merchant would have given us twelve roubles for a broadcloth (and he said he would have had them all) and four altines for a pound of sugar, but we did refuse it because he was the first, and the merchants were not come thither, nor would not come before winter, trusting to have more; but I fear it will not be much better; yet, notwithstanding, we did for the best. And the house that our wares lie in cost from that day until Easter ten roubles. And the 28th day of September we did determine with ourselves that it was good for Masters Gray, Arthur Edwards, Thomas Hattery, Christopher Hudson, John Sedgewicke, Richard Johnson, and Richard Good, to tarry at Vologda, and Masters Chanceler, Henry Lane, Edward Prise, Robert Best, and I, should go to Moscow. And we did lade the Emperor's sugar, with part of all sorts of wares to have had to the Moscow with us, and the way was so deep that we were fain to turn back and leave it still at Vologda till the frost. And we went forth with post-horse, and the charge of every horse, being still ten in number, comes to 10s. 7.5d., besides the guides; and we came to the Moscow the fourth day of October, and were lodged that night in a simple house; but the next day we were sent for to the Emperor his secretary, and he bade us welcome with a cheerful countenance and cheerful words, and we showed him that we had a letter from our Queen's grace to the Emperor his grace, and then he desired to see them all (and that they might remain with him, to have them perfect, that the true meaning might be declared to the Emperor), and so we did; and then we were appointed to a better house; and the seventh day the secretary sent for us again, and then he showed us that we should have a better house, for it was the Emperor his will that we should have all things that we did lack, and did send us mead of two sorts, and two hens, our house free, and every two days to receive eight hens, seven altines, and twopence in money and medow and a certain poor fellow to make clean our house and to do that whereunto we should set him; and we had given many rewards before, which you shall perceive by other, and so we gave the messengers a reward with thanks; and the ninth day we were sent to make us ready to speak with the Emperor on the morrow. And the letters were sent us that we might deliver them ourselves, and we came before him the tenth day; and before we came to his presence we went through a great chamber, where stood many small tons, pails, bowls, and pots of silver (I mean like washingbowls), all parcel gilt; and within that another chamber, wherein sat (I think) near a hundred in cloth of gold, and then into the chamber where his grace sat, and there, I think, were more than in the other chamber, also in cloth of gold; and we did our duty, and showed his grace our Queen's grace's letters, with a note of your present which was left in Vologda, and then his grace did ask how our Queen's grace did, calling her cousin, saying that he was glad that we were come in health into his realm, and we went one by one unto him and took him by the hand, and then his grace did bid us go in health, and come to dinner again; and we dined in his presence, and were set with our faces towards his grace, and none in the chamber sat with their backs towards him, being, I think, near a hundred at dinner then, and all served with gold as platters, chargers, pots, cups, and all not slender, but very massive, and yet a great number of platters of gold, standing still on the cupboard, not moved. And divers times in the dinner- time his grace sent us meat and drink from his own table; and when we had dined we went up to his grace and received a cup with drink at his own hand, and the same night his grace sent certain gentlemen to us with divers sorts of wine and medow, to whom we gave a reward. And afterwards we were by divers Italians counselled to take heed whom we did trust to make the copy of the privileges that we would desire to have for fear it should not be written in the Russian tongue, as we did mean. So first, a Russian did write for us a breviate to the Emperor, the tenour whereof was, that we did desire a stronger privilege. And when the secretary saw it he did deliver it to his grace; and when we came again his grace willed us to write our minds, and he would see it, and so we did. And his grace is so troubled with preparations to wars that as yet we have no answer. But we have been required of his secretary, and of the under- chancellor, to know what wares we have brought into the realm, and what wares we do intend to have that are or may be had in this realm. And we showed them; that they showed the Emperor thereof. And then they said his grace's pleasure was that his best merchants of the Moscow should be spoken to to meet and talk with us. And so a day was appointed, and we met in the secretary his office, and there was the under-chancellor, who was not past two years since the Emperor's merchant, and not his chancellor. And then the conclusion of our talk was that the chancellor willed us to bethink us where we would desire to have a house or houses, that we might come to them as to our own house, and for merchandise to be made preparation for us, and they would know our prices of our wares and frise. And we answered, that for our prices they must see the wares before we could make any price thereof, for the like in goodness had not been brought into the realm, and we did look for an example of all sorts of our wares to come from Vologda with the first sled way, and then they should see them, and then we would show them the prices of them. And likewise we could not tell them what we would give them justly till we did know as well their just weight as their measures (for in all places where we did come all weights and measures did vary). Then the secretary (who had made promise unto us before) said that we should have all the just measures under seal, and he that was found faulty in the contrary to buy or sell — with any other measure than that, the law, was that he should be punished. He said, moreover, that if it so happen that any of our merchants do promise by covenant at any time to deliver you any certain sum of wares in such a place, and of such like goodness, at such a day, for such a certain price, that then because of variance we should cause it to be written, according as the bargain is, before a justice or the next ruler to the place. If he did not keep covenant and promise in all points, according to his covenant, that then look what loss or hindrance we could justly prove that we have thereby, he should make it good if he be worth so much. And in like case we must do to them; and to that we did agree, save only if it were to come over the sea, then if any such fortune should be (as God forbid) that the ship should mischance or be robbed, and the proof to be made that such kind of wares were laden, the English merchants to bear no loss to the other merchant. Then the chancellor said, "Methinks you shall do best to have your house at Colmogro, which is but one hundred miles from the right discharge of the ships; and yet I trust the ships shall come nearer hereafter, because the ships may not tarry long for their lading, which is one thousand miles from Vologda by water, and all our merchants shall bring all our merchandise to Colmogro to you, and so shall our merchants neither go empty nor come empty. For if that they lack lading homeward, there is salt, which is good ware here, that they may come laden again." So we were very glad to hear that, and did agree to his saying. For we shall, nevertheless, if we list, have a house at Vologda and at the Moscow, yea, and at Novogrod, or where we will in Russland. But the three-and-twentieth of this present we were with the secretary, and then among other talk we moved, that if we should tarry at Colmogro with our wares, and should not come to Vologda, or, further, to seek our market, but tarry still at Colmogro, and then the merchants of the Moscow and others should not come and bring their wares, and so the ships should come, and not have their lading ready, that then it were a great loss and hindrance for us. Then said he again to us, that the merchants had been again together with him, and had put the like doubt that if they should come and bring their wares to Colmogro, and that they should not find wares there sufficient to serve them, that then they should be at great loss and hindrance, they leaving their other trades to fall to that. And to that we did answer, that after the time that we do appoint with them to bring their wares to Colmogro, God willing, they should never come thither but at the beginning of the year, they should find that our merchants would have at the least for a thousand roubles, although the ships were not come. So that he said, that then we must talk further with the merchants. So that as yet I know not but that we shall have need of one house at Colmogro and another at Vologda, and if that they bring not their wares to Colmogro, then we shall be sure to buy some at Vologda, and to be out of bondage.

And thus may we continue three or four years, and in this space we shall know the country and the merchants, and which way to save ourselves best, and where to plant our houses, and where to seek for wares. For the Moscow is not best for any kind of wares for us to buy, save only wax, which we cannot have under sevenpence the Russian pound, and it lacks two ounces of our pound; neither will it be much better cheap, for I have bidden sixpence for a pound. And I have bought more—five hundred weight of yarn—which stands me in eightpence farthing the Russian pound, one with another. And if we had received any store of money, and were dispatched here of that we tarry for, as I doubt not but we shall be shortly (you know what I mean), then as soon as we have made sail, I do intend to go to Novogrod and to Pletsco, whence all the great number of the best tow flax cometh, and such wares as are there I trust to buy part. And fear you not, we will do that may be done, if God send us health; desiring you to prepare fully for one ship to be ready in the beginning of April to depart off the coast of England.

Concerning all those things which we have done in the wares you shall receive a perfect note by the next bearer (God willing), for he that carrieth these from us is a merchant of Turwell, and he was caused to carry these by the commandment of the Emperor, his secretary, whose name is Evan Mecallawiche Weskawate, whom we take to be our very friend. And if it please you to send any letters to Dantiske, to Robert Elson, or to William Watson's servant, Dunstan Walton to be conveyed to us, it may please you to enclose ours in a letter sent from you to him, written in Polish, Dutch, Latin, or Italian; so enclosed coming to the Moscow to his hands, he will convey our letters to us wheresoever we be. And I have written to Dantiske already to them for the conveyance of letters from thence.

And to certify you of the weather here, men say, that these three hundred years was never so warm weather in this country at this time of the year. But as yesternight we received a letter from Christopher Hudson from a city called Yereslave, who is coming hither with certain of our wares, but the winter did deceive him, so that he was fain to tarry by the way; and he wrote that the Emperor's present was delivered to a gentleman at Vologda, and the sled did overthrow, and the butte of Hollocke was lost, which made us all very sorry.

I pray you be not offended with these my rude letters, for lack of time; but as soon as sales be made I will find the means to convey you a letter with speed; for the way is made so doubtful, that the right messenger is so much in doubt, that he would not have any letters of any effect sent by any man if he might, for he knows not of these; and to say the truth, the way is not for him to crawl in. But I will make another shift beside, which I trust shall serve the turn till he come, if sales be made before he be ready, which is and shall be as pleaseth God; Who ever preserve your worship, and send us good sales. Written in haste,

By yours to command,

GEORGE KILLINGWORTH, Draper.

Certain Instructions delivered in the Third Voyage, Anno 1556, for Russia, to every Purser and the rest of the Servants, taken for the Voyage, which may serve as good and necessary Directions to all other like Adventurers.

1. First, you shall, before the ship doth begin to lade, go aboard, and shall there take and write one inventory by the advice of the master, or of some other principal officer, there aboard, of all the

tackle, apparel, cables, anchors, ordnance, chambers, shot, powder, artillery, and of all other necessaries whatsoever doth belong to the said ship; and the same justly taken you shall write in a book, making the said master, or such officer, privy of that which you have so written, so that the same may not be denied when they shall call account thereof. That done, you shall write a copy of the same with your own hand, which you shall deliver before the ship shall depart for the voyage, to the company's bookkeeper, here to be kept to their behalf, to the end that they may be justly answered the same when time shall require; and this order to be seen and kept every voyage orderly, by the pursers of the company's own ship in any wise.

2. Also, when the ship beginneth to lade, you shall be ready aboard with your book to enter such goods as shall be brought aboard to be laden for the company, packed or unpacked, taking the marks and numbers of every pack, fardell, truss, or packet, coronoya, chest, vat, butt, pipe, puncheon, whole barrel, half barrel, firkin, or other cask, maunde, or basket, or any other thing which may or shall be packed by any other manner of way or device. And first, all such packs or trusses, etc., as shall be brought aboard to be laden not marked by the company's mark, you shall do the best to let that the same be not laden, and to inquire diligently to know the owners thereof, if you can, and what commodity the same is that is so brought aboard to be laden; if you cannot know the owners of such goods learn what you can thereof, as well making a note in your book, as also to send or bring word thereof to the agent, and to some one of the four merchants with him adjoined so speedily as you can, if it be here laden, or to be laden in this river, being not marked with the company's mark, as is aforesaid; and when the said ship hath received in all that the company's agent will have laden, you shall make a just copy of that which is laden, reciting the parcels, the marks and numbers of everything plainly, which you shall likewise deliver to the said bookkeeper to the use aforesaid.

3. Also, when the ship is ready to depart, you shall come for your cockets and letters to the agent, and shall show him all such letters as you have received of any person or persons privately or openly, to be delivered to any person or persons in Russia or elsewhere, and also to declare if you know any other that shall pass in the ship

either master or mariner that hath received any letters to be privily delivered to any there, directed from any person or persons, other than from the agent here to the agent there; which letters so by you received, you shall not carry with you, without you be licensed so to do by the agent here, and some of the four merchants as is afore-said; and such others as do pass, having received any privy letters to be delivered, you shall all that in you lieth let the delivery of them at your arriving in Russia; and also if you have, or do receive, or shall know any other that doth or hath received any goods of ready money to be employed in Russia, or to be delivered there to any person or persons from any person or persons other than such as be the company's goods, and that under their mark, you shall, before the ship cloth depart, declare the same truly to the said agent, and to some of the other merchants to him adjoined, as it is before declared.

4. Also, when the ship is ready to depart, and hath the master and the whole company aboard, you shall diligently foresee and take heed, that there pass not any privy person or persons, other than such as be authorised to pass in the said ship, without the licence and warrant of one of the governors and of the assistants, for the same his passage, to be first shown. And if there be any such person or persons that is to pass and will pass without showing the same warrant, you shall let the passage of any such to the uttermost of your power; and for that there may no such privy person pass un-der the cloak and colour of some mariner, you shall upon the weighing of your ship's anchor call the master and the mariners within board by their names, and that by your books, to the end that you may see that you have neither more nor less, but just the num-ber for the voyage.

5. Also, you must have in remembrance that if it shall chance the ship to be put into any harbour in this coast by contrary winds, or otherwise in making the voyage, to send word thereof from time to time as the case shall require, by your letters in this manner: "To Master I. B., Agent for the Company of the New Trades in S. in London." If you do hire any to bring your letters, write that which he must have for the postage. And for your better knowledge and learning, you shall do very well to keep a daily note of the voyage both outwards and homewards.

6. And principally see that you forget not daily in all the voyage, both morning and evening, to call the company within board to prayer, in which doing you shall please God, and the voyage will have the better success thereby and the company prosper the better.

7. Also in calm weather and at other times when you shall fortune to come to anchor in the seas during the voyage, you shall for the company's profit, and for good husbanding of the victuals aboard, call upon the boatswain and other of the company to use such hooks and other engines as they have aboard to take fish with, that such fish so taken may be eaten for the cause aforesaid; and if there be no such engines aboard, then to provide some before you go from hence.

8. And when God shall send you in safety into the Bay of St. Nicholas at anchor, you shall go ashore with the first boat that shall depart from the ship, taking with you such letters as you have to deliver to the agent there: and if he be not there at your coming ashore, then send the company's letters to Colmogro to him by some sure mariner or otherwise, as the master and you shall think best; but go not yourself at any hand, nor yet from aboard the ship unless it be ashore to treat with the agent for the lading of the ship that you be appointed in, which you shall apply diligently to have done so speedily as may be. And for the discharging of the goods therein in the bay, to be carried from thence, see that you do look well to the unlading thereof, that there be none other goods sent ashore than the company's, and according to the notes entered in your book as aforesaid: if there be, inquire diligently for whom they be, and what goods they be, noting who is the receiver of the said goods, in such sort that the company may have the true knowledge thereof at your coming home.

9. Also there ashore, and likewise aboard, you shall spy, and search as secretly as you may, to learn and know what bargaining, buying, and selling there is with the master and mariners of the ship, and the Russians, or with the company's servants there; and that which you shall perceive and learn you shall keep a note thereof in your book, secretly to yourself, which you shall open and disclose at your coming home, to the governors and the assistants, in such sort as the truth of their secret trades and occupyings may be

revealed and known. You shall need always to have Argus' eyes, to spy their secret packing and conveyance, as well on land as aboard the ship, of and for such furs, and other commodities, as yearly they do use to buy, pack, and convey hither. If you will be vigilant and secret in this article, you cannot miss to spy their privy packing one with another, either on shore or aboard the ship; work herein wisely, and you shall deserve great thanks of the whole country.

10. Also at the lading again of the ship, you shall continue and abide aboard, to the end that you may note and write in your book all such goods and merchandise as shall be brought and laden, which you shall orderly note in all sorts as heretofore, as in the second article partly it is touched; and in any wise, put the master and the company in remembrance to look and foresee substantially to the roomaging of the ship, by fair means or threats, as you shall see and think will serve for the best.

11. Thus, when the ship is fully laden again, and all things aboard in good order, and that you do fortune to go ashore to the agent for your letters, and despatch away, you shall demand whether all the goods be laden that were brought thither, and to know the truth thereof you shall repair to the company's storehouse there, at St. Nicholas, to see if there be any goods left in the said storehouse; if there be, you shall demand why they be not had laden, and to note what kind of goods they be, that be so left; and seeing any of the ships there, not fully laden, you shall put the agent in remembrance to lade those goods so left, if any such be to be laden, as is aforesaid. And thus, God sending you a fair wind, to make speed and away.

12. Finally, when God shall send you to arrive again upon this coast in safety, either at Harwich or elsewhere, go not you ashore, if you may possible, to the end that when you be gone ashore there may no goods be sent privily ashore to be sold, or else to be sold aboard the ship in your absence, but keep you still aboard, if you can by any means, for the causes aforesaid, and write the company a letter from the ship of your good arrival, which you may convey to them by land, by some boy or mariner of the ship, or otherwise as you shall think best and likewise when God shall send you and the ship into the river here, do not in any wise depart out of the ship

that you be in, until the company do send some other aboard the ship, in your stead and place, to keep the said ship in your absence.

A DISCOURSE

Of the honourable receiving into England of the first Ambassador from the Emperor of Russia, in the year of Christ 1556, and in the third year of the reign of Queen Mary, serving for the third voyage to Moscow. — Registered by Master John Incent, Protonotarie.

It is here recorded by writing and authentical testimony, partly for memory of things done and partly for the verity to be known to posterity in time to come, that whereas the Most High and Mighty Ivan Vasivilich, Emperor of all Russia, Great Duke of Volidemer, Muscovy and Novogrode, Emperor of Cassan and of Astrachan, Lord of Piskie, and Great Duke of Smolenski, Tverski, Yowgoriski, Permiski, Viatski, Boligarski, and Sibieriski, Emperor and Great Duke of many others, as Novogrode in the Nether Countries, Charnogoski, Rizanski, Volodski, Rezewski, Bielski, Rostoski, Yeraslavski, Bialazarski, Woodarski, Opdorski, Condinski, and many other countries, and lord over all those parts in the year of our Lord God ensuing, the account of the Latin Church, 1556, sent by the sea from the Port of St. Nicholas, in Russia, his Right honourable Ambassador, surnamed Osepp Napea, his high officer in the town and country of Vologhda, to the most famous and excellent Princes, Philip and Mary, by the grace of God King and Queen of England, Spain, France, and Ireland, Defenders of the Faith, Archdukes of Austria, Dukes of Burgundy, Milan, and Brabant, counties of Hasburge, Flanders, and Tyrol, his ambassador and orator, with certain letters tenderly conceived, together with certain presents and gifts mentioned in the foot of this memorial, as a manifest argument and token of a mutual amity and friendship to be made and continued between their Majesties and subjects respectively, for the commodity and benefit of both the realms and people; which orator was the 20th day of July embarked and shipped in and upon a good English ship named the Edward Bonaventura, belonging to the Governor, Consuls, and company of English merchants, Richard Chanceler being grand pilot, and John Buckland master of the said ship, in which was laden, at the adventure of the aforesaid ambassador and merchants, at several accounts, goods and merchandise, viz., in wax, train oil, tallow, furs, felts, yarn, and such-like, to the sum of 20,000 li. sterling, together with sixteen Russians, attendant upon the person of the said ambassador—over and above ten other Russians shipped within the said Bay of St. Nicholas in one other good ship, to the said company also belonging, called the Bona Speranza, with goods of the said orators and merchants to the value of 6,000 li. sterling as by the invoices and letters of lading of the said several ships (whereunto relation is to be had) particularly appeareth; which good ships, coming in good order into the seas, and traversing the same in their journey towards the coast of England, were by contrary winds and extreme tempest of weather severed the one from the other; that is to say, the said Bona Speranza, with two other English ships, also appertaining to the said company, the one surnamed the Philip and Mary, the other the Confidentia, were driven on the coast of Norway into Drenton Water, where the said Confidentia was seen to perish on a rock, and the other, videlicet the Bona Speranza, with her whole company, being to the number of four-and-twenty persons, seemed to winter there, whereof no certainty at this present day is known. The third, videlicet the Philip and Mary, arrived in the Thames nigh London the eighteenth day of April, in the year of our Lord 1557. The Edward Bonaventura, traversing the seas for months, finally, the tenth day of November, of the aforesaid year of our Lord 1556, arrived within the Scottish coast in a bay named Pettislego, where, by outrageous tempests and extreme storms, the said ship, being beaten from her ground tackles, was driven upon the rocks on shore, where she broke and split in pieces; in such sort as the grand pilot, using all carefulness for the safety of the body of the ambassador and his train, taking the boat of the said ship, trusting to attain the shore and so to save and preserve the body, and seven of the company or attendants of the said ambassador, the same boat by rigorous waves of the seas was by dark night overwhelmed and drowned, wherein perished, not only the body of the said grand pilot, with seven Russians, but also divers of the mariners of the said ship; the noble personage of the said ambassador, with a few others (by God's preservation and special favour), only with much difficulty saved. In which shipwreck, not only the said ship was broken, but also the whole mass and body of the goods laden in her was, by the rude and ravenous people of the country thereunto adjoining, rifled, spoiled, and carried away, to the manifest loss and utter destruction of all the lading of the said ship, and together with the ship, apparel, ordnance, and furniture, belonging to the company, in value of 1,000 pounds of all, which was not restored towards the costs and charges to the sum of 500 li. sterling.

As soon as by letters addressed to the said company, and in London delivered the 6th of December last past, it was to them certainly known of the loss of their pilot, men, goods, and ship, the same merchants with all celerity and expedition obtained, not only the Queen's Majesty's most gracious and favourable letters to the Lady Dowager and Lords of the Council of Scotland for the gentle comfortment and entertainment of the said ambassador, his train and company, with preservation and restitution of his goods, as in such miserable cases to Christian pity, princely honour, and mere justice appertaineth, but also addressed two gentlemen of good learning, bravity, and estimation, videlicet Master Lawrence Hussie, Doctor of the Civil Law, and George Gilpin, with money and other requisites, into the realm of Scotland, to comfort, aid, assist, and relieve him and his there, and also to conduct the ambassador into England, sending with them by post a talmack or speechman, for the better furniture of the service of the said ambassador, trusting thereby to have the more ample and speedy redress of restitution; which personages, using diligence, arrived at Edinburgh (where the Queen's Court was) the three-and-twentieth day of the said month of December, who, first visiting the said ambassador, declaring the causes of their coming and commission, showing the letters addressed in his favour, the order given them for his solace and furniture of all such things as he would have, together with their daily and ready service to attend upon his person and affairs, repaired consequently to the Dowager Queen, delivering the letters.

Whereupon they received gentle answers with hope and comfort of speedy restitution of the goods, apparel, jewels, and letters; for the more apparance whereof the Queen sent first certain commissioners with a herald of arms to Pettislego, the place of the ship-wreck, commanding by proclamation and other edicts all such persons (no degree excepted) as had any part of such goods as were spoiled and taken out or from the ship, to bring them in, and to restore the same with such further order as Her Grace by advice of her council thought expedient; by reason whereof, not without great labours, pains, and charges, (after a long time) divers small parcels of wax, and other small trifling things of no value, were by the poorer sort of the Scots brought to the commissioners; but the jewels, rich apparel, presents, gold, silver, costly furs, and such- like, were conveyed away, concealed, and utterly embezzled. Whereupon the Queen, at the request of the said ambassador, caused divers persons, to the number of one hundred and eighty or more, to be called personally before her princely presence to answer to the said spoil, and really to exhibit and bring in all such things as were spoiled and violently taken, and carried out of the same, whereof not only good testimony by writing was shown, but also the things themselves found in the hands of the Scottish subjects, who by subtle and crafty dealings, by connivance of the commissioners, so used (or rather abused) themselves towards the same orator and his attendants, that in effectual restitution was made; but he, wearied with daily attendance and charges, the 14th day of February next ensuing, distrusting any real and effectual rendering of the said goods and merchandises and other the premises, upon leave obtained of the said Queen, departed towards England, having attending upon him the said two English gentlemen and others (leaving, nevertheless, in Scotland three Englishmen to pursue the delivery of such things as were collected to have been sent by ship to him into England, which being in April next, and not before, embarked for London, was not at this present day here arrived), came the 18th day of February to Barwike (Berwick) within the dominion and realm of England, where he was by the Queen's Majesty's letters and commandment honourably received, used, and entertained by the Right Honourable Lord Wharton, Lord Warden of the East Marches, with goodly conducting from place to place as the daily journeys done ordinarily did lie, in such order, manner, and form as to a personage of such estate appertaineth. He, prosecuting his voyage until the 27th of February, approached the City of London within twelve English miles, where he was received with fourscore merchants with chains of gold and goodly apparel, as well in order of men- servants in one uniform livery, as also in and upon good horses and geldings, who conducting him to a merchant's house four miles from London, received there a quantity of gold, velvet, and silk, with all furniture thereunto requisite, wherewith he made him a riding garment, reposing himself that night. The next day being Saturday, and the last day of February, he was by the merchants adventuring for Russia, to the number of one hundred and forty persons, and so many or more servants in one livery as above said, conducted towards the City of London, where by the way he had not only the hunting of the fox and such-like sport shown him, but also by the Queen's Majesty's commandment was received and embraced by the Right Honourable Viscount Montagu, sent by her Grace for his entertainment. He being accompanied with divers lusty knights, esquires, gentlemen, and yeomen to the number of three hundred horses, led him to the north parts of the City of London, where by four notable merchants, rich apparelled, was presented to him a right fair and large gelding, richly trapped, together with a foot- cloth of Orient crimson velvet, enriched with gold laces, all furnished in most glorious fashion, of the present and the gift of the said merchants; whereupon the ambassador at instant desire mounted, riding on the way towards Smithfield Bars, the first limits of the liberties of the City of London. The Lord Mayor, accompanied with all the aldermen in their scarlet, did receive him; and so riding through the City of London in the middle between the said Lord Mayor and Viscount Montagu, a great number of merchants and notable personages riding before, and a large troop of servants and apprentices following, was conducted through the City of London (with great admiration and plausibility of the people, running plentifully on all sides, and replenishing all streets in such sort as no man without difficulty might pass) into his lodging situate in Fant Church (Fenchurch) Street, where were provided for him two chambers richly hung and decked over and above the gallant furniture of the whole house, together with an ample and rich cupboard of plate of all sorts, to furnish and serve him at all meals and other services during his abode in London, which was, as is underwritten, until the third day of May; during which time, daily, divers aldermen and the gravest personages of the said company did visit him, providing all kinds of victuals for his table and his servants, with all sorts of officers to attend upon him in good sort and condition, as to such an ambassador of honour doth and ought to appertain.

It is also to be remembered that, at his first entrance into his chamber, there was presented unto him on the Queen's Majesty's behalf for a gift and present, and his better furniture in apparel, one rich piece of cloth of tissue, a piece of cloth of gold, another piece of cloth of gold raised with crimson velvet, a piece of crimson velvet ingrained, a piece of purple velvet, a piece of damask purpled, a piece of crimson damask, which he most thankfully accepted. In this beautiful lodging, refreshing and preparing himself and his train with things requisite, he abode expecting the King's Majesty's repair out of Flanders into England; whose Highness arriving the one-and-twentieth of March, the same ambassador the five-and-twentieth of March, being the Annunciation of Our Lady (the day twelvemonth he took his leave from the Emperor his master), was most honourably brought to the King's and Queen's Majesty's Court at Westminster, where, accompanied first with the said viscount and other notable personages and the merchants, he arriving at Westminster Bridge, was there received with six lords, conducted into a stately chamber, where by the Lords Chancellor, Treasurer, Privy Seal, Admiral, Bishop of Ely, and other councillors, he was visited and saluted; and consequently was brought unto the King's and Queen's Majesty's presence, sitting under a stately cloth of honour, the chamber most richly decked and furnished, and most honourably presented. Where, after that he had delivered his letters, made his oration, given two timber of sables, and the report of the same both in English and Spanish, in most loving manner embraced, was with much honour and high entertainment, in sight of a great confluence of people, lords and ladies, soon after remitted by water to his former lodging, to the which, within two days after, by assignment of the King's and Queen's Majesties, repaired and conferred with him secretly two grave councillors—that is, the Lord Bishop of Ely and Sir William Peter Knight, Chief Secretary to their Highnesses, who, after divers secret talks and conference, reported to their Highnesses their proceedings, the gravity, wisdom, and stately behaviour of the said ambassador, in such sort as was much to their Majesties' satisfaction.

Finally, concluding upon such treaties and articles of amity as the letters of the King's and Queen's Majesties most graciously, under the Great Seal of England, to him by the said councillors delivered, doth appear.

The four-and-twentieth of April, being the Feast of St. George wherein was celebrated the solemnity of the Noble Order of the Gaiter at Westminster, the same lord ambassador was soon after required to have an audience; and therefore conducted from the said lodging to the Court by the Right Noble the Lords Talbot and Lumley to their Majesties' presence, where (after his oration made, and thanks both given and received) he most honourably took his leave, with commendations to the Emperor, which being done, he was with special honour led unto the chapel, where, before the King and Queen's Majesties, in sight of the whole Order of the Garter, was prepared for him a stately seat, wherein he, accompanied with the Duke of Norfolk, the lords last above mentioned, and many other honourable personages, was present at the whole service, in ceremonies which were to him most acceptable. The divine service ended, he was quickly remitted and reduced to his barge, and so repaired to his lodgings in like order and gratulation of the people universally as before.

The time of the year hasting the departure of the ambassador, the merchants having prepared four goodly and well-trimmed ships laden with all kinds of merchandise apt for Russia, the same ambassador making provision for such things as him pleased, the same ships in good order valed (sailed?) down the river of Thames from London to Gravesend, where the same ambassador, with his train and furniture, was embarked towards his voyage homeward, which Cod prosper in all felicity.

It is also to be remembered that during the whole abode of the said ambassador in England the agents of the said merchants did not only prosecute and pursue the matter of restitution in Scotland, and caused such things to be laden in an English ship hired purposely to convey the ambassador's goods to London, there to be delivered to him, but also, during his abode in London, did both invite him to the mayor and divers worshipful men's houses, feasting and banqueting him right friendly, showing unto him the most notable and commendable sights of London, as the King's Palace and house, the Churches of Westminster and Paul's, the Tower and Guild Hall of London, and such-like memorable spectacles. And, also, the said nine-and-twentieth day of April the said merchants, assembling themselves together in the house of the Drapers' Hall of London, exhibited and gave unto the said ambassador a notable supper garnished with music, interludes, and banquets, in the which a cup of wine being drunk to him in the name and lieu of the whole company, it was signified to him that the whole company, with most liberal and friendly hearts, did frankly give to him and his all manner of costs and charges and victuals, riding from Scotland to London during his abode there, and until setting of sail aboard the ship, requesting him to accept the same in good part, as a testimony and witness of their good hearts, zeal, and tenderness towards him and his country.

It is to be considered that of the Bona Speranza no word nor knowledge was had at this present day, nor yet of the arrival of the ships or goods from Scotland.

The third of May the ambassador departed from London to Gravesend, accompanied with divers aldermen and merchants, who in good guard set him aboard the noble ship the Primrose, admiral to the fleet, where leave was taken on both sides and parts, after many embracements and divers farewells, not without expressing of tears.

Memorandum, that the first day of May the councillors, videlicet the Bishop of Ely and Sir William Peter, on behalf of the King's and Queen's Majesties, repairing to the Lord Ambassador, did not only deliver unto him their Highnesses' letters of recommendation under the Great Seal of England to the Emperor, very tenderly and friendly written, but also, on their Majesties' behalf, gave and delivered certain notable presents to the Emperor's person, and also gifts for the Lord Ambassador's proper use and behoof, as by the particulars under-written appeareth, with such further good words and commendations as the more friendly have not been heard; whereby it appeareth how well affected their honours be to have and continue amity and traffic between their honours and their subjects; which thing as the King's and Queen's Majesties have shown of their princely munificences and liberalities, so have likewise the merchants and fellowship of the adventurers for and to Russia manifested to the world their good-wills, minds, and zeals borne to this new-commenced voyage, as by the discourse above mentioned, and other the notable acts overlong to be recited in this present memorial, doth and may most clearly appear, the like whereof is not in any precedent or history to be shown.

Forasmuch as it may be doubted how the ship named the Edward Bonaventura received shipwreck, what became of the goods, how much they were spoiled and detained, how little restored, what charges and expenses ensued, what personages were drowned, how the rest of the ships either arrived or perished, or how the disposition of Almighty God had wrought His pleasure in them; how the same ambassador hath been after the miserable case of shipwreck in Scotland irreverently abused, and consequently into England received and conducted, there entertained, used, honoured, and, finally, in good safety towards his return and repair furnished, and with much liberality and frank handling friendly dismissed, to the intent that the truth of the premises may be to the Most Mighty Emperor of Russia sincerely signified in eschewment of all events and misfortunes that may chance in this voyage (which God defend!) to the ambassador's person, train, and goods, this present memorial is written and authentically made, and by the said ambassador, his servants whose names be under-written, and train, in presence of the notary, and witnesses under-named, recognised, and acknowledged. Given the day, month, and year under-written, of which instrument into every of the said ships one testimonial is delivered, and the first remaineth with the said company in London.

Gifts sent to the King and Queen's Majesties of England by the Emperor of Russia, by the report of the Ambassador, and spoiled by the Scots after the Shipwreck.

1. First, six timber of sables rich in colour and hair.

2. Item, twenty entire sables exceeding beautiful with teeth, ears, and claws.

3. Item, four living sables with chains and collars.

4. Item, thirty Lausannes large and beautiful.

5. Item, six large and great skins, very rich and rare, worn only by the Emperor for worthiness.

6. Item, a large and fair white Jerfawcon, for the wild swan, crane, goose, and other great fowls. Together with a drum of silver, the hoops gilt, used for a lure to call the said hawk.

Gifts sent to the Emperor of Russia by the King and Queen's Majesties of England.

1. First, two rich pieces of cloth of tissue.

2. Item, one fine piece of scarlet.

3. Item, one fine violet in grain.

4. Item, one fine azure cloth.

5. Item, a notable pair of brigandines, with a murrian covered with crimson velvet and gilt nails.

6. Item, a male and female lions.

Gifts given to the Ambassador at his Departure, over and above such as were delivered unto him at his first Arrival.

1. First, a chain of gold of one hundred pound.

2. Item, a large basin and ewer, silver and gilt.

3. Item, a pair of pottle pots gilt.

4. Item, a pair of flagons gilt.

THE VOYAGE Wherein OSEPP NAPEA, the Muscovite Ambassador, returned home into his Country, with his Entertainment at his Arrival at Colmogro; and a large description of the Manners of the Country.

The 12th of May, in the year of our Lord 1567, there departed from Gravesend four good ships, well appointed for merchants, which were presently bound into the Bay of St. Nicholas in Russia, with which ships were transported or carried home one Osepp Gregoriwich Napea, who was sent messenger from the Emperor and Great Duke of Muscovy. The four ships were these whose names follow, viz.

The Primrose, Admiral.
The John Evangelist, Vice-Admiral.
The Anne, and the Trinity, Attendants.

The 13th of July, the aforesaid four ships came to an anchor in the Bay of St. Nicholas, before an Abbey called the Abbey of St. Nicholas, whereas the said messenger, Osepp Gregoriwich Napea, went ashore, and as many Englishmen as came to serve the Emperor, remained with him at the Abbey, for the space of six days, until he had gotten all his things ashore, and laden the same in barques to go up the river Dwina, unto Vologhda, which is by water 1,000 verstes, and every verste is about three-quarters of an English mile.

The 20th of July, we departed from St. Nicholas, and the 24th of the same we came to Colmogro, where we remained eight days; and the same messenger was there of all his acquaintance welcomed home, and had presents innumerable sent unto him, but it was nothing but meat and drink; some sent white bread, some rye bread, and some buttered bread and pancakes, beef, mutton, bacon, eggs, butter, fishes, swans, geese, ducks, hens, and all manner of victuals—both fish and flesh—in the best manner that the rude people could devise; for among them these presents are highly esteemed.

The 29th of July we departed from Colmogro, and the 14th of August we came to Vstioug, where we remained one day, and changed our barques, or boats.

The 27th of August we came to Vologhda, where we remained four days, unlading the barques, and lading our chests and things in small waggons, with one horse in a piece — which in their tongue are called "telegos"; and these telegos, they carried our stuff from Vologhda unto the Moscow, which is 500 verstes; and we were upon the same way fourteen days; for we went no faster than the telegos.

There are three great towns between the Moscow and Vologhda — that is to say, Yereslava, Rostave, and Pereslava. Upon one side of Yereslava runneth a famous river, which is called Volga. It runneth into the Caspian Sea, and it divideth itself, before it come into the Mare Caspium, in fifty parts or more: and near unto the same sea there stands a great city called Boghare; the inhabitants of the which are called by the same name.

The people of the said city do traffic in the city of Moscow: their commodities are spices, musk, ambergris, rhubarb, with other drugs. They bring also many furs, which they buy in Siberia, coming towards the Moscow. The said people are of the sect of Mahomet.

The 12th of September we came unto the city of Moscow, where we were brought by Napea and two of the Emperor's gentlemen unto a large house, where every one of us had his chamber appointed.

The 14th of September we were commanded to come unto the Emperor, and immediately after our coming we were brought into his presence, unto whom each of us did his duty accordingly, and kissed his right hand, his Majesty sitting in his chair of state, with his crown on his head and a staff of goldsmith's work in his left hand well garnished with rich and costly stones; and when we had all kissed his hand and done our duty, his Majesty did declare by his interpreter that we were all welcome unto him, and into his country, and thereupon willed us to dine with him that day. We gave thanks unto his Majesty, and so departed until the dinner was ready.

When dinner-time approached we were brought again into the Emperor's dining chamber, where we were set on one side of a table that stood over against the Emperor's table, to the end that he might well behold us all, and when we came into the aforesaid chamber we found there ready set these tables following:-

First, at the upper end of one table were set the Emperor's Majesty, his brother, and the Emperor of Cassan, who is prisoner. About two yards lower sat the Emperor of Cassan's son, being a child of five years of age, and beneath him sat the most part of the Emperor's noblemen.

And at another table near unto the Emperor's table there was set a monk all alone, who was in all points as well served as the Emperor. At another table sat another kind of people called Chirkasses, which the Emperor entertaineth for men of war to serve against his enemies; of which people and of their country I will hereafter make mention.

All the tables aforesaid were covered only within salt and bread, and after that we had sat awhile, the Emperor sent unto every one of us a piece of bread, which was given and delivered unto every man severally with these words: "The Emperor and Great Duke giveth thee bread this day;" and in like manner three or four times before dinner was ended he sent unto every man drink, which was given with these words: "The Emperor and Great Duke giveth thee to drink." All the tables aforesaid were served in vessels of pure and fine gold, as well basins and ewers, platters, dishes, and saucers, as also of great pots, with an innumerable sort of small drinking-pots of divers fashions, whereof a great number were set with stone. As for costly meats, I have many times seen better; but for change of wines, and divers sorts of meads, it was wonderful; for there was not left at any time so much void room on the table that one cup more might have been set, and as far as I could perceive all the rest were in the like manner served.

In the dinner-time there came in six singers who stood in the midst of the chamber, and their faces towards the Emperor, who sang there before dinner was ended three several times, whose songs or voices delighted our ears little or nothing.

The Emperor never putteth morsel of meat in his mouth but he first blesseth it himself, and in like manner as often as he drinketh; for after his manner he is very religious, and he esteemeth his religious persons above his noblemen.

This dinner continued about the space of five hours, which being ended, and the tables taken up, we came into the midst of the chamber, where we did reverence unto the Emperor's Majesty, and then he delivered unto every one of us with his own hands a cup of mead, which when every man had received and drunk a quantity thereof we were licensed to depart, and so ended that dinner. And because the Emperor would have us to be merry, he sent to our lodging the same evening three barrels of mead of sundry sort, of the quantity in all of one hogshead.

The 16th day of September the Emperor sent home unto our lodging for every one of us a Tartary horse to ride from place to place as we had occasion, for that the streets of Moscow are very foul and miry in the summer.

The 18th of September there were given unto Master Standish, doctor in physic, and the rest of our men of our occupations, certain furred gowns of branched velvet and gold, and some of red damask, of which Master Doctor's gown was furred with sables, and the rest were furred, some with white ermine, and some with grey squirrel, and all faced and edged round about with black beaver.

The 1st of October, in the morning, we were commanded to come unto the Emperor's Court, and when we came thither we were brought unto the Emperor, unto whom we did our duties accordingly, whereupon he willed us to dine with him that day, and so with thanks unto his Majesty we departed until dinner-time, at which time we came and found the tables covered with bread and salt as at the first; and after that we were all set upon one side of the table, the Emperor's Majesty according to his accustomed manner sent unto every man of us a piece of bread by some of the dukes who attended upon his Highness.

And whereas the 14th of September we were served in vessels of gold, we were now served in vessels of silver, and yet not so abundantly as was the first of gold; they brought drink unto the table in silver bowls, which contained at the least six gallons apiece, and every man had a small silver cup to drink in, and another to dip or to take his drink out of the great bowl withal. The dinner being ended, the Emperor gave unto every one of us a cup with mead, which when we had received, we gave thanks and departed.

Moreover, whensoever the Emperor's pleasure is that any stranger shall dine with him, he doth send for them in the morning, and when they come before him, he with his own mouth biddeth them to dinner, and this order he always observeth.

The 10th of October the Emperor gave unto Master Standish seventy roubles in money and to the rest of our men of occupations thirty roubles apiece.

The 3rd of November we dined again with the Emperor, where we were served as before.

The 6th of December being St. Nicholas' Day, we dined again at the Emperor's, for that is one of the principal feasts which the Muscovites hold. We were served in silver vessels, and ordered in all points as before, and it was past seven of the clock at night before dinner was ended.

The Emperor's Majesty useth every year in the month of December to have all his ordnance that is in the city of Moscow carried into the fields which are without the suburbs of the city, and there to have it planted and bent upon two houses of wood filled within with earth. Against which two houses there were two fair white marks set up, at which marks they discharge all their ordnance, to the end the Emperor may see what his gunners can do. They have fair ordnance of brass of all sorts-bases, falcons, minions, sakers, culverins, cannons (double and royal), basilisks (long and large); they have six great pieces, whose shot is a yard of height, which shot a man may easily discern as they flee. They have also a great many of mortar pieces or pot guns, out of which pieces they shoot wild fire.

The 12th of December the Emperor's Majesty and all his nobility came into the field on horse-back in most goodly order, having very fine jennets and Turkey horses garnished with gold and silver abundantly; the Emperor's Majesty having on him a gown of rich tissue and a cap of scarlet on his head, set not only with pearls, but also with a great number of rich and costly stones; his noblemen were all in gowns of cloth of gold, who did ride before him in good order by three and three, and before them there went 5,000 arquebusiers, which went by five and five in a rank in very good order, every of them carrying his gun upon his left shoulder and his match in his right hand, and in this order they marched into the field where the aforesaid ordnance was planted.

And before the Emperor's Majesty came into the field there was a certain stage made of small poles, which was a quarter of a mile long, and about three score yards off from the stage of poles were certain pieces of ice of two feet thick and six feet high set up, which rank of ice was as long as the stage of poles; and as soon as the Emperor's Majesty came into the field, the arquebusiers went upon the stage of poles, where they settled themselves in order. And when the Emperor's Majesty was settled where he would be, and where he might see all the ordnance discharged and shot off, the arquebusiers began to shoot off at the bank of ice as though it had been in any skirmish or battle, who ceased not shooting until they had beaten all the ice flat on the ground.

After the hand-guns, they shot off their wild fire up into the air, which was a goodly sight to behold. And after this they began to discharge the small pieces of brass, beginning with the smallest, and so orderly bigger and bigger, until the last and biggest. When they had shot them all off, they began to charge them again, and so shot them all off three times after the first order, beginning with the smallest and ending with the greatest. And note that before they had ended their shooting, the two houses that they shot unto were beaten in pieces, and yet they were very strongly made of wood and filled with earth, being at the least thirty feet thick. This triumph being ended, the Emperor departed and rode home in the same order that he came forth into the field. The ordnance is discharged every year in the month of December, according to the order before mentioned.

On Christmas Day we were all willed to dine with the Emperor's Majesty, where for bread, meat, and drink we were served as at other times before. But for goodly and rich plate we never saw the like or so much before. There dined that day in the Emperor's presence above 500 strangers and 200 Russians, and all they were served in vessels of gold, and that as much as could stand one by another upon the tables. Besides this there were four cupboards garnished with goodly plate, both of gold and silver. Among the which there were twelve barrels of silver containing above twelve gallons apiece, and at each end of every barrel were six hoops of fine gold. This dinner continued about six hours.

Every year upon the Twelfth Day they use to bless or sanctify the river Moska, which runneth through the city of Moscow (Moscovia), after this manner:-

First, they make a square hole in the ice about three fathoms large every way, which is trimmed about the sides and edges with white boards. Then about nine of the clock they come out of the church with procession towards the river in this wise:-

First and foremost there go certain young men with wax tapers burning, and one carrying a great lantern. Then follow certain banners, then the cross, then the images of Our Lady and St. Nicholas, and of other saints, which images men carry upon their shoulders. After the images follow certain priests to the number of 100 or more. After them the Metropolitan, who is led between two priests; and after the Metropolitan came the Emperor, with his crown upon his head, and after his Majesty all his noblemen orderly. Thus they followed the procession unto the water, and when they came unto the hole that was made, the priests set themselves in order round about it. And at one side of the same pool there was a scaffold of boards made, upon which stood a fair chair, in which the Metropolitan was set, but the Emperor's Majesty stood upon the ice.

After this the priests began to sing, to bless, and to cense, and did their service, and so by the time that they had done the water was holy, which being sanctified, the Metropolitan took a little thereof in his hands and cast it on the Emperor, likewise upon certain of the dukes, and then they returned again to the church with the priests that sat about the water; but the press that there was about the water when the Emperor was gone was wonderful to behold, for there came above 5,000 pots to be filled of that water. For that Muscovite which hath no part of that water thinks himself unhappy.

And very many went naked into the water, both men, women, and children. After the press was a little gone, the Emperor's jennets and horses were brought to drink of the same water, and likewise many other men brought their horses thither to drink, and by that means they make their horses as holy as themselves.

All these ceremonies being ended, we went to the Emperor to dinner, where we were served in vessels of silver, and in all other points as we had been beforetime.

The Russians begin their Lent always eight weeks before Easter: the first week they eat eggs, milk, cheese, and butter, and make great cheer with pancakes and such other things, one friend visiting another, and from the same Sunday until our Shrove Sunday there are but few Russians sober; but they are drunk day by day, and it is accounted for no reproach or shame among them.

The next week, being our first week of Lent, or our cleansing week, beginning our Shrove Sunday, they make and keep a great fast. It is reported, and the people do verily believe, that the Metropolitan neither eateth nor drinketh any manner of thing for the space of seven days; and they say that there are many religious men who do the like.

The Emperor's Majesty eateth but one morsel of bread and drinketh but one draught of drink but once in the day during that week, and all men that are of any reputation come not out of their houses during that time; so that the streets are almost void of company, saving a few poor folk who wander to and fro. The other six weeks they keep as we do ours, but not one of them will eat either butter, cheese, eggs, or milk.

On Palm Sunday they have a very solemn procession in this manner following:-

First, they have a tree of a good bigness, which is made fast upon two sleds, as though it were growing there, and it is hung with apples, raisins, figs, and dates, and with many other fruits abundantly. In the midst of the same tree stand five boys in white vestures, which sing in the tree before the procession. After this there followed certain young men with wax tapers in their hands burning and a great lantern, that all the light should not go out; after them followed two with long banners, and six with round plates set upon long staves (the plates were of copper, very full of holes, and thin); then followed six carrying painted images upon their shoulders; after the images follow certain priests to the number of one hundred or more, with goodly vestures, whereof ten or twelve are of white damask set and embroidered round about with fair and Orient pearls as great as peas, and among them certain sapphires and other stones. After them followed the one-half of the Emperor's noblemen; then cometh the Emperor's Majesty and the Metropolitan, after this manner:-

First, there is a horse covered with white linen cloth down to the ground, his ears being made long with the same cloth like to an ass's ears. Upon this horse the Metropolitan sitteth sidelong, like a woman; in his lap lieth a fair book, with a crucifix of goldsmith's work upon the cover, which he holdeth fast with his left hand; and in his right hand he has a cross of gold, with which cross he ceaseth not to bless the people as he rideth.

There are, to the number of thirty, men who spread abroad their garments before the horse, and as soon as the horse is passed over any of them they take them up again and run before and spread them again, so that the horse doth always go on some of them. They who spread the garments are all priests' sons, and for their labours the Emperor giveth unto them new garments.

One of the Emperor's noblemen leadeth the horse by the head, but the Emperor himself, going on foot, leadeth the horse by the end of the rein of his bridle with one of his hands, and in the other of his hands he had a branch of a palm-tree; after this followed the rest of the Emperor's noblemen and gentlemen, with a great number of other people. In this order they went from one church to another within the castle, about the distance of two flights' shot; and so returned again to the Emperor's church, where they made an end of their service; which being done, the Emperor's Majesty and certain of his noblemen went to the Metropolitan's house to dinner, where of delicate fishes and good drinks there was no lack.

The rest of this week until Easter Day they keep very solemnly, continuing in their houses for the most part; and upon Monday or Thursday the Emperor doth always use to receive the Sacrament, and so doth most part of his nobles.

Upon Good Friday they continue all the day in contemplation and prayers, and they use every year on Good Friday to let loose a prisoner in the stead of Barabbas. The night following they go to the church, where they sleep unto the next morning; and at Easter they have the Resurrection, and after every of the Lents they eat flesh the next week following Friday, Saturday and all.

They have an order at Easter which they always observe, and that is this:- Every year, against Easter, to dye or colour red with brazil a great number of eggs of which every man and woman giveth one unto the priest of their parish upon Easter Day, in the morning; and, moreover, the common people use to carry in their hands one of these red eggs, not only upon Easter Day, but also three or four days after; and gentlemen and gentlewomen have eggs gilded, which they carry in like manner. They use it, as they say, for a great love, and in token of the Resurrection, whereof they rejoice; for when two friends meet during the Easter holidays, they come and take one another by the hand: the one of them saith, "The Lord or Christ is risen," the other answereth, "It is so, of a truth;" and then they kiss and exchange their eggs (both men and women), continuing in kissing four days together.

The 12th of April being Tuesday in the Easter week, Master Jenkinson and Master Gray and certain other of us Englishmen dined with the Emperor, where we were served as we had been beforetime. And after dinner the Emperor's Majesty gave unto Master Jenkinson and unto Master Gray, and so orderly unto every one of us, a cup of mead, according to his accustomed manner, which when every man had received and given thanks, Master Jenkinson stepped into the midst of the chamber before the Emperor's Majesty and gave thanks to his Highness for his goodness unto him extended, desiring his Grace to license him for to depart; and in like manner did Master Gray. His Majesty did not only license them to depart, but also granted unto Master Jenkinson his letters, under his Great Seal, unto all princes through whose dominions Master Jenkinson should have occasion to pass, that he might the sooner and quietlier pass by means thereof. Which being granted, Masters Jenkinson and Gray lowly submitted themselves, thanking his Majesty. So the Emperor gave unto either of them a cup of mead to drink, and willed them to depart at their pleasure in God's peace.

The 14th of April, in the morning, when Master Gray and I were ready to depart towards England, the Chancellors sent unto us, and willed us to come to their office in the Chancery, where at our coming they showed us a great number of the Emperor's jewels and rich robes, willing us to mark and behold them well, to the end that at our arrival into England we might make report what we had seen there.

The chiefest was his Majesty's crown, being close under the top very fair wrought; in mine opinion, the workmanship of so much gold few men can amend. It was adorned and decked with rich and precious stones abundantly, among the which one was a ruby, which stood a handful higher than the top of the crown upon a small wire; it was as big as a good bean. The same crown was lined with a fair black sable worth by report forty roubles.

We saw all his Majesty's robes, which were very richly set with stones; they showed us many other great stones of divers kinds, but the most part of these were uneven, in manner as they came out of the work, for they do more esteem the greatness of stones than they do the proportion of them.

We saw two goodly gowns, which were as heavy as a man could easily carry, all set with pearls over and over; the guards or borders round about them were garnished with sapphires and other good stones abundantly. One of the same gowns was very rich, for the pearls were very large, round, and Orient. As for the rest of his gowns and garments, they were of rich tissue and cloth-of-gold, and all furred with very black sables.

When we had sufficiently perused all these things, they willed Master Gray, at his arrival in England, to provide, if he could, such jewels and rich clothes as he had seen there, and better if he could, declaring that the Emperor would gladly bestow his money upon such things.

So we took our leave the same time, and departed towards Vologhda immediately.

THE MANNERS, USAGES, AND CEREMONIES OF THE RUSSIANS

OF THE EMPEROR.

The Emperor's name in their tongue is Evan Vasilivich; that is as much as to say, John, the son of Vasilie. And by his princely state he is called Otesara, as his predecessors have been before; which, to interpret, is "A King that giveth not tribute to any man." And this word Otesara, his Majesty's interpreters have of late days interpreted to be an Emperor; so that now he is called Emperor and Great Duke of all Russia, &c. Before his father, they were neither called Emperors nor Kings, but only Ruese Velike; that is to say, Great Duke. And as this Emperor, which now is Ivan Vasilivich, doth exceed his predecessors in name—that is, from a Duke to an Emperor- -even so much by report he doth exceed them in stoutness of courage and valiantness, and a great deal more: for he is no more afraid of his enemies, which are not a few, than the hobby of the larks.

His enemies with whom he hath wars for the most part are these:- Litto Poland, Sweden, Denmark, Lifland, the Crimmes, Nagaians, and the whole nation of the Tartarians, which are a stout and a hardy people as any under the sun.

This Emperor useth great familiarity, as well unto all his nobles and subjects, as also unto Strangers which serve him either in his wars or in occupations: for his pleasure is that they shall dine oftentimes in the year in his presence; and, besides that, he is oftentimes abroad, either at one church or another, and walking with his noblemen abroad. And by this means he is not only beloved of his nobles and commons, but also had in great dread and fear through all his dominions, so that I think no prince in Christendom is more feared of his own than he is, nor yet better beloved. For if he bid any of his dukes go, they will run; if he give any evil or angry word to any of them, the party will not come into his Majesty's presence again for a long time if he be not sent for, but will feign him to be very sick, and will let the hair of his head grow very long, without either cutting or shaving, which is an evident token that he is in the Emperor's displeasure; for when they be in their prosperity, they account it a shame to wear long hair — in consideration whereof they use to have their heads shaven.

His Majesty heareth all complaints himself, and with his own mouth giveth sentence and judgment of all matters, and that with expedition; but religious matters he meddleth not withal, but referreth them wholly unto the Metropolitan.

His Majesty retaineth and well rewardeth all strangers that come to serve him, and especially men of war.

He delighteth not greatly in hawking, hunting, or any other pastime, nor in hearing instruments or music, but setteth all his whole delight upon two things: first, to serve God, as undoubtedly he is very devout in his religion; and the second, how to subdue and conquer his enemies.

He hath abundance of gold and silver in his own hands or treasury; but the most part of his know not a crown from a counter, nor gold from copper — they are so much cumbered (combred) therewithal; and he that is worth two, three, or four groats is a rich man.

OF THEIR RELIGIOUS MEN.

The Metropolitan is next unto God, Our Lady and St. Nicholas excepted; for the Emperor's Majesty judgeth and affirmeth him to be of higher dignity than himself: "For that," saith he, "he is God's spiritual officer, and I, the Emperor, am His temporal officer;" and therefore his Majesty submitteth himself unto him in many things concerning religious matters, as in leading the Metropolitan horse upon Palm Sunday, and giving him leave to sit on a chair upon the Twelfth Day, when the river Moscow was in blessing, and his Majesty standing on the ice.

All matters of religion are reformed by the Metropolitan: he heareth the causes and giveth sentence as himself listeth, and is authorised so to do. Whether it be to whip, hang, or burn, his will must needs be fulfilled.

They have both monks, friars, and nuns, with a great number of great and rich monasteries; they keep great hospitality, and do relieve much poor people day by day. I have been in one of the monasteries called Troities, which is walled about with brick very strongly, like a castle, and much ordnance of brass upon the walls of the same. They told me themselves that they are seven hundred brethren of them which belong unto that house. The most part of the lands, towns, and villages which are within forty miles of it belong unto the same. They showed me the church, wherein were as many images as could hang about, or upon the walls of the church roundabout; and even the roof of the church was painted full of images. The chief image was of Our Lady, which was garnished with gold, rubies, sapphires, and other rich stones abundantly. In the midst of the church stood twelve wax tapers of two yards long, and a fathom about in bigness. There stands a kettle full of wax, with about one hundredweight, wherein there is always the wick of a candle burning- -as it were, a lamp which goeth not out day nor night.

They showed me a coffin, covered with cloth-of-gold, which stood upon one side within their church, in which they told me lay a holy man, who never ate nor drank, and yet he liveth. And they told me (supposing that I had believed them) that he healeth many diseases, and giveth the blind their sight, with many other miracles; but I was hard of belief, because I saw him work no miracle whilst I was there.

After this they brought me into their cellars, and made me taste of divers kinds of drinks, both wine and beer, mead and quassia, of sundry colours and kinds. Such abundance of drink as they have in their cellars, I do suppose few princes have more, or so much at once.

Their barrels or vessels are of an unmeasurable bigness and size, some of them are three yards long and more, and two yards and more broad in their heads. They contain six or seven tons apiece.

They have none in their cellars of their own making that are less than a ton. They have nine or ten great vaults, which are full of those barrels, which are seldom removed, for they have trunks which come down through the roof of the vaults in sundry places, through which they pour the drink down, having the cask right under it to receive the same, for it should be a great trouble to bring it all down the stairs.

They give bread, meat, and drink unto all men that come to them, not only while they are at their abbey, but also when they depart, to serve them by the way.

There are a great number of such monasteries in the realm, and the Emperor's Majesty rideth oftentimes from one to another of them, and lieth at them three or four days together.

The same monks are as great merchants as any in the land of Russia, and do occupy buying and selling as much as any other men, and have boats which pass to and fro in the rivers with merchandise from place to place where any other of their country do traffic.

They eat no flesh during their lives, as it is reported; but upon Sunday, Monday, Tuesday, Thursday, and Saturday, it is lawful for them to eat eggs, butter, cheese, and milk, and at all times to eat fish; and after this sort they lead their lives.

They wear all black garments, and so do none other in all the land, but at that abbey only.

They have no preachers—no, not one in all the land to instruct the people, so that there are many, and the most part of the poor in the country, who if one ask them how many gods there be, they will say a great many, meaning that every image which they have is a god; for all the country and the Emperor's Majesty himself will bless and bow and knock their heads before their images, insomuch that they will cry earnestly unto their images to help them to the things which they need. All men are bound by their law to have those images in their houses; and over every gate in all their towns and cities are images set up, unto which the people bow and bend, and knock their heads against the ground before them. As often as they come by any church or cross, they do in like manner. And when they come to any house, they bless themselves three or four times before they will salute any man in the house.

They reckon and hold it for great sin to touch or handle any of their images within the circle of the board where the painting is, but they keep them very daintily, and rich men deck them over and about with gold, silver, and stones, and hang them over and about with cloth-of-gold.

The priests are married as other men are, and wear all their garments as other men do, except their night-cap, which is cloth of some sad colour, being round, and reacheth unto the ears; their crowns are shaven, but the rest of their hair they let grow as long as Nature will permit, so that it hangeth beneath their ears upon their shoulders; their beards they never shave. If his wife happen to die, it is not lawful for him to marry again during his life.

They minister the Communion with bread and wine, after our order, but he breaketh the bread and putteth it into the cup unto the wine, and commonly some are partakers with them; and they take the bread out again with a spoon, together with part of the wine, and so take it themselves, and give it to others that receive with them after the same manner.

Their ceremonies are all, as they say, according to the Greek Church, used at this present day; and they allow no other religion but the Greeks' and their own, and will not permit any nation but the Greeks to be buried in their sacred burials or churchyards.

All their churches are full of images, unto the which the people, when they assemble, do bow and knock their heads, as I have before said, that some will have knobs upon their foreheads, with knocking, as great as eggs.

All their service is in the Russian tongue, and they and the common people have no other prayers but this, "Ghospodi Jesus Christos esine voze ponuloi nashe." That is to say, "O Lord Jesus Christ, Son of God, have mercy upon us;" and this is their prayer, so that the most part of the unlearned know neither Paternoster, nor the Belief, nor Ten Commandments, nor scarcely understand the one-half of the service which is read in their churches.

OF THEIR BAPTISM.

When any child is born, it is not baptised until the next Sunday; and if it chance that it be not baptised then, it must tarry until the second Sunday after the birth. And it is lawful for them to take as many godfathers and godmothers as they will; the more the better.

When they go to the church, the midwife goeth foremost, carrying the child; and the godfathers and godmothers follow into the midst of the church, where there is a small table ready set, and on it an earthen pot full of warm water, about the which the godfathers and godmothers with the child settle themselves. Then the clerk giveth unto every of them a small wax candle burning; then cometh the priest, and beginneth to say certain words which the godfathers and godmothers must answer word for word, among which one is, that the child shall forsake the Devil, and as that name is pronounced, they must all spit at the word, as often as it is repeated. Then he blesseth the water which is in the pot, and doth breathe over it; then he taketh all the candles which the gossips have, and, holding them all in one hand, letteth part of them drop into the water, and then giveth every one his candle again. And when the water is sanctified he taketh the child and holdeth it in a small tub, and one of the godfathers taketh the pot with warm water, and poureth it all upon the child's head.

After this, he hath many more ceremonies — as anointing ears and eyes with spittle, and making certain crosses with oil upon the back, head, and breast of the child; then, taking the child in his arms, carrieth it to the images of St. Nicholas and Our Lady, &c., and speaketh unto the images, desiring them to take charge of the child, that he may live and believe as a Christian man or woman ought to do, with many other words. Then, coming back from the images, he taketh a pair of shears and clippeth the young and tender hairs of the child's head in three or four places; and then delivereth the child, whereunto every of the godfathers and godmothers lays a hand. Then the priest chargeth them that the child be brought up in the faith and fear of God or Christ, and that it be instructed to cling and bow to the images, and so they make an end. Then one of the godfathers must hang a cross about the neck of the child, which he must always wear; for that Russian who hath not a cross about his neck, they esteem as no Christian man; and thereupon they say that we are no Christians, because we do not wear crosses as they do.

OF THEIR MATRIMONY.

Their matrimony is nothing solemnised, but rather in most points abominable, and, as near as I can learn, in this wise following:-

First, when there is love between the parties, the man sendeth unto the woman a small chest or box, wherein is a whip, needles, thread, silk, linen-cloth, shears, and such necessaries as she shall occupy when she is a wife; and perhaps sendeth therewithal raisins, figs, or some such things—giving her to understand that, if she do offend, she must be beaten with the whip; and by the needles, thread, cloth, &c., that she should apply herself diligently to sew, and do such things as she could best do; and by the raisins or fruits he meaneth, if she do well, no good thing shall be withdrawn from her, nor be too dear for her. And she sendeth unto him a shirt, handkerchiefs, and some such things of her own making. And now to the effect.

When they are agreed, and the day of marriage appointed, when they shall go towards the church, the bride will in no wise consent to go out of the house, but resisteth and striveth with them that would have her out, and feigneth herself to weep; yet in the end two women get her out, and lead her towards the church, her face being covered close, because of her dissimulation, that it should not be openly perceived; for she maketh a great noise, as though she were sobbing and weeping, until she come at the church, and then her face is uncovered. The man cometh after, among other of his friends, and they carry with them to the church a great pot with wine or mead. Then the priest coupleth them together, much after our order, one promising to love and serve the other during their lives together, &c.; which being done, they begin to drink. And first the woman drinketh to the man, and when he hath drunk he letteth the cup fall to the ground, hasting immediately to tread upon it, and so doth she, and the one who treads first upon it must have the victory and be master at all times after, which commonly happeneth to the man, for he is readiest to set his foot on it, because he letteth it fall himself. Then they go home again, the woman's face being uncovered. The boys in the streets cry out and make a noise in the meantime with very dishonest words.

When they come home, the wife is set at the upper end of the table, and the husband next unto her. They fall then to drinking, till they be all drunk; they perchance have a minstrel or two. And two naked men, who led her from the church, dance naked a long time before all the company. When they are weary of drinking, the bride and the bridegroom get them to bed (for it is in the evening always when any of them are married); and when they are going to bed, the bridegroom putteth certain money — both gold and silver, if he have it — into one of his boots, and then sitteth down in the chamber, crossing his legs; and then the bride must pluck off one of his boots, which she will, and if she happen on the boot wherein the money is, she hath not only the money for her labour, but is also at such choice as she need not ever from that day forth to pull off his boots; but if she miss the boot wherein the money is, she doth not only lose the money, but is also bound from that day forwards to pull off his boots continually.

Then they continue in drinking and making good cheer three days following, being accompanied with certain of their friends; and during the same three days he is called a duke, and she a duchess, although they be very poor persons. And this is as much as I have learned of their matrimony; but one common rule is amongst them — if the woman be not beaten with the whip once a week, she will not be good, and therefore they look for it orderly; and the women say that if their husbands did not beat them, they should not love them.

They use to marry there very young — their sons at sixteen and eighteen years old, and the daughters at twelve or thirteen years, or younger. They use to keep their wives very closely — I mean, those that be of any reputation; so that a man shall not see one of them but at a chance, when she goeth to church at Christmas or at Easter, or else going to visit some of her friends.

The most part of the women use to ride astride in saddles with stirrups, as men do, and some of them on sleds, which in summer is not commendable.

The husband is bound to find the wife colours to paint her withal, for they use ordinarily to paint themselves; it is such a common practice among them that it is counted for no shame. They grease their faces with such colours that a man may discern them hanging on their faces almost a fight-shot off. I cannot so well liken them as to a miller's wife, for they look as though they were beaten about the face with a bag of meal; but their eyebrows they colour as black as jet.

The best property that the women have, is that they can sew well, and embroider with silk and gold excellently.

OF THEIR BURIAL.

When any man or woman dieth, they stretch him out, and put a new pair of shoes on his feet, because he hath a great journey to go; then do they wind him in a sheet, as we do; but they forget not to put a testimony in his right hand, which the priest giveth him to testify unto St. Nicholas that he died a Christian man or woman. And they put the corse always in a coffin of wood, although the party be very poor—and when they go towards the church, the friends and kinsmen of the party departed carry in their hands small wax candles, and they weep and howl and make much lamentation.

They that be hanged or beheaded, or suchlike, have no testimony with them; how they are received into heaven, it is a wonder, without their passport.

There are a great number of poor people among them who die daily for lack of sustenance, which is a pitiful case to behold; for there hath been buried in a small time, within these two years, above eighty persons young and old, who have died only for lack of sustenance; for if they had straw and water enough, they would make shift to live; for a great many are forced in the winter to dry straw and stamp it, and to make bread thereof — or, at the least, they eat it instead of bread. In the summer they make good shift with grass, herbs, and roots; barks of trees is good meat with them at all times. There is no people in the world, as I suppose, that live so miserably as do the poor in those parts; and the most part of them that have sufficient for themselves, and also to relieve others that need, are so unmerciful that they care not how many they see die of famine or hunger in the streets.

It is a country full of diseases, divers and evil; and the best remedy is for any of them, as they hold opinion, to go often unto the hothouses, as a manner every man hath one of his own, which he heateth commonly twice every week, and all the household sweat and wash themselves therein.

THE VOYAGES OF OHTHERE AND WULFSTAN
To the White Sea and to the Mouth of the Vistula in the Time of Alfred the Great, with Notes on the Geography of Europe inserted by
KING ALFRED, In his Translation of Orosius.

KING ALFRED'S OROSIUS. (FROM "ENGLISH WRITERS.")

One of King Alfred's labours for the enlightenment of his countrymen was a translation of the "Universal History of Orosius, from the Creation to the year of our Lord 416." This book had long been in high repute by the familiar name of "Orosius" among students and teachers in the monasteries; and it retained its credit so, that after the invention of printing it was one of the first works put into type, and appeared in numerous editions. The author was a Spanish Christian of the fifth century. Born at Tarragona and educated in Spain, he crossed over to Africa about the year 414, and received instruction from St. Augustine upon knotty questions of the origin of the soul and other matters. In Augustine's works are contained the "Consultation of Orosius with Augustine on the Error of the Priscillianists and Origenists," and a letter from Augustine to Orosius against them. Augustine sent Orosius to consult Jerome, who was in Palestine; and in his letter of introduction said, "Behold, there has come to me a religious young man, in catholic peace a brother, in age a son, in rank a co-presbyter, Orosius—of active talents, ready eloquence, ardent application, longing to be in God's house a vessel useful for disproving false and destructive doctrines, which have killed the souls of Spaniards much more grievously than the barbarian sword their bodies." In Palestine, towards the latter half of the year 415, Orosius attacked the Pelagians by writing against them a treatise on Free Will, and presenting a memorial against them to the Council of Diospolis. It was at the request of St Augustine that Orosius wrote his History. The sack of Rome by Alaric having caused the Christians of Rome to doubt the efficacy of their faith, Augustine, while he himself wrote his "De Civitate Dei" to show from the history of the Church that the preaching of the Gospel could not augment the world's misery, incited Orosius to show the same thing in a compendium of profane history also. Orosius began his work in the year 410, when Augustine had got through ten books of his, and he finished it about the year 416. Like a good old-fashioned controversialist, he made very light of the argument of terror from the sack of Rome by Alaric, so representing the event that King Alfred, in his translation, thus abridged the detail:-

"Alaric, the most Christian and the mildest of kings, sacked Rome with so little violence, that he ordered no man should be slain, and that nothing should be taken away or injured that was in the churches. Soon after that, on the third day, they went out of the city of their own accord. There was not a single house burnt by their order."

In translating and adapting this book to the uses of his time, King Alfred did not trouble himself at all with its old ecclesiastical character, as what Pope Gelasius I. had called a book written "with wonderful brevity against heathen perversions. Looking to it exclusively as a digest of historical and geographical information, Alfred abridged, omitted, imitated, added, with a single regard to his purpose of producing a text-book of that class of knowledge. Omitting the end of the fifth book and the beginning of the sixth, and so running two books into one, he made the next and last book the sixth instead of the seventh, as it is in the original.

The "History of Orosius" itself is bald, confused; but it was enriched and improved by Alfred's addition to the first book of much new matter, enlarging knowledge of the geography of Europe, which he calls Germania, north of the Rhine and Danube. Alfred adds also to the same book geographical narratives taken from the lips of two travellers. One was Ohthere, a Norwegian, who sailed from Halgoland, on the coast of Norway, round the North Cape into the Cwen-Sae, or White Sea, and entered the mouth of the river Dwina, the voyage ending where there is now Archangel, the most northern of the Russian seaports. Ohthere afterwards made a second voyage from Halgoland along the west and south coast of Norway to the Bay of Christiania, and Sciringeshael, the port of Skerin, or Skien, near the entrance of the Christiania fjord. He then sailed southward, and reached in five days the Danish port aet

Haedum, the capital town called Sleswic by the Saxons, but by the Danes Haithaby. The other traveller was Wulfstan, who sailed in the Baltic, from Slesvig in Denmark to Frische Haff within the Gulf of Danzig, reaching the Drausen Sea by Elbing. These voyages were taken from the travellers' own lips. Of Wulfstan's, the narrative passes at one time into the form of direct personal narration — "Wulfstan said that he went . . . that he had . . . And then we had on our left the land of the Burgundians [Bornholmians], who had their own king. After the land of the Burgundians we had on our left," &c. The narrative of the other voyage opens with the sentence, "Ohthere told his lord, King Alfred." These three additions to "Orosius" — the Description of Europe, the two voyages of Ohthere, and the voyage of Wulfstan — may be considered Alfred's own works.

The Description is the king's own account of Europe in his time, and the only authentic record of the Germanic nations, written by a contemporary, so early as the ninth century.

Ohthere was a man of great wealth and influence in Norway, as wealth was there reckoned; for he had 600 reindeer, including six decoy- deer; but though accounted one of the first men in the land, he had only twenty horned cattle, twenty sheep, and twenty swine. The little that he ploughed he ploughed with horses, and his chief revenue was in tribute of skin and bone from the Finns. The fame of his voyages attracted to him the attention of King Alfred. He said that he dwelt "Northmost of all northmen," in Halgoland; and wishing to find out how far the land lay due north, and whether any man dwelt north of him — for the sake also of taking the walruses, "which have very good bone in their teeth; of these teeth they brought some to the king; and their hides are very good for ship-ropes" — he sailed northward. Ohthere may have obtained some of his wealth by whale-fishing. He says that "in his own country is the best whale- hunting; they are eight-and-forty ells long, and the largest fifty ells long;" of these he said "that he was one of six who killed sixty in two days;" meaning, no doubt, that his vessel was one of six. He relates only what he saw. "The Biarmians," he says, "told him many stories both about their own land and about the countries which were around them, but he knew not what was true, because he did not see it himself."

Wulfstan was perhaps a Jutlander, and his voyage was confined to the Baltic. Neither his account nor that of Ohthere contradicts the opinion then held, that Scandinavia was a large island, and the Gulf of Bothnia or Cwaener Sea flowed into the North Sea.

94

THE GEOGRAPHY OF EUROPE BY KING AL-FRED, ETC.

Translated in 1807 by the Rev. James Ingram, M.A., Professor of Anglo-Saxon at the University of Oxford.

Now will we describe the geography of Europe, so far, at least, as our knowledge of it extends. From the river Tanais, westward to the river Rine (which takes its rise from the Alps and runs directly north thenceforward on to the arm of the ocean that surrounds Bryttania), then southward to the river Danube (whose source is near the river Rine, running afterwards in its course along the confines of Northern Greece, till it empties itself into the Mediterranean), and northward even unto the ocean, which men call Cwen-sea; within these boundaries are many nations; but the whole of this tract of country is called Germany.

Then to the north of the source of the Danube, and to the east of the Rine, are the Eastern Franks, and to the south of them are the Suabians; on the opposite bank of the Danube, and to the south and east, are the Bavarians, in that part which is called Regnesburh. Due east from thence are the Bohemians, and to the north-east the Thyringians, to the north of these are the Old Saxons, to the north- west are the Frieslanders, and to the west of the Old Saxons is the mouth of the Elbe, as also Friesland. Hence to the west-north is that land which is called Angleland, Sealand, and some part of Den- marc; to the north is Apdrede, and to the east-north the wolds, which are called the Heath-wolds. Hence eastward is the land of the Veneti (who are also called Silesae), extending south-west over a great part of the territory of the Moravians. These Moravians have to the west the Thyringians and Bohemians, as also part of Bavaria, and to the south, on the other side of the Danube, is the country of the Carinthians, lying southward even to the Alps. To the same mountains also extend the boundaries of the Bavarians and the Suabians. Thence to the eastward of Carinthia, beyond the waste, is the land of the Bulgarians. To the east of them is the land of the Greeks, and to the east of Moravia is Wisle-land; to the east of that are the Dacae, who were originally a tribe of Goths. To the north-east of the Moravians are the Dalamensae; east of the Dalamensians are the Horithi, and north of the Dalamensians are the Servians; to the west also are the Silesians. To the north of the Horiti is Mazovia, and north of Mazovia are the Sarmatians, quite to the Riphaean mountains. To the west of the Southern Danes is the arm of the ocean that surrounds Britannia, and to the north of them is the arm of the sea called Ost Sea; to the east and to the north of them are the Northern Danes, both on the continent and on the islands; to the east of them are the Afdrede; and to the south is the mouth of the Elb, with some part of Old Saxony. The Northern Danes have to the north of them the same arm of the sea called Ost Sea; to the east of them is the nation of the Estonians, and the Afdrede to the south. The Estonians have to the north of them the same arm of the sea, and also the Winedae and Burgundae, and to the South are the Heath-wolds. The Burgundians have the same arm of the sea to the west of them, and the Sweons to the north; to the east of them are the Sarmatians, and to the south the Servians. The Sweons have to the south of them the same arm of the sea, called Ost Sea; to the east of them the Sarmatians; and to the north, over the wastes, is Cwenland; to the west-north of them are the Scride- Finnas, and to the west the Northmen.

"Ohthere told his lord, King Alfred, that he lived to the north of all the Northmen. He says that he dwelt on the mainland to the northward, by the west sea; that the land, however, extends to a very great length thence onward to the north; but it is all waste, except in a few places where the Finlanders occasionally resort, for hunting in the winter, and in the summer for fishing along the sea-coast. He said that he was determined to find out, on a certain time, how far this country extended northward, or whether any one lived to the north of the waste. With this intent he proceeded northward along the coast, leaving all the way the waste land on the starboard, and the wide sea on the backboard, for three days. He was then as far north as the whale-hunters ever go. He then continued his voyage, steering yet northward, as far as he could sail within three other days. Then the land began to take a turn to the eastward, even unto the inland sea, but he knows not how much farther. He remembers, however, that he stayed there waiting for a western wind, or a point to the north, and sailed thence eastward by the land as far as he could in four days. Then he was obliged to wait for a due north wind, because the land there began to run southward, quite to the inland sea; he knows not how far. He sailed thence along the coast southward, as far as he could in five days. There lay then a great river a long way up in the land, into the mouth of which they entered, because they durst not proceed beyond the river from an apprehension of hostilities, for the land was all inhabited on the other side of the river. Ohthere, however, had not met with any inhabited land before this since he first set out from his own home. All the land to his right, during his whole voyage, was uncultivated and without inhabitants, except a few fishermen, fowlers, and hunters, all of whom were Finlanders; and he had nothing but the wide sea on his left all the way. The Biarmians, indeed, had well cultivated their land; though Ohthere and his crew durst not enter upon it; but the land of the Torne-Finnas was all waste, and it was only occasionally inhabited by hunters, and fishermen, and fowlers.

"The Biarmians told him many stories, both about their own land and about the other countries around them; but Ohthere knew not how much truth there was in them, because he had not an opportunity of seeing with his own eyes. It seemed, however, to him, that the Finlanders and the Biarmians spoke nearly the same language. The principal object of his voyage, indeed, was already gained; which was, to increase the discovery of the land, and on account of the horse- whales, because they have very beautiful bone in their teeth, some of which they brought to the king, and their hides are good for ship-ropes. This sort of whale is much less than the other kinds, it is not longer commonly than seven ells: but in his own country (Ohthere says) is the best whale-hunting; there the whales are eight and forty ells long, and the largest fifty; of these, he said, he once killed (six in company) sixty in two days. He was a very rich man in the possession of those animals, in which their principal wealth consists, namely, such as are naturally wild. He had then, when he came to seek King Alfred, six hundred deer, all tamed by himself, and not purchased. They call them reindeer. Of these six were stall-reins, or decoy deer, which are very valuable amongst the Finlanders, because they catch the wild deer with them.

"Ohthere himself was amongst the first men in the land, though he had not more than twenty rother-beasts, twenty sheep, and twenty swine; and what little he ploughed, he ploughed with horses. The annual revenue of these people consists chiefly in a certain tribute which the Finlanders yield them. This tribute is derived from the skins of animals, feathers of various birds, whalebone, and ship-ropes, which are made of whales' hides and of seals. Everyone pays according to his substance; the wealthiest man amongst them pays only the skins of fifteen marterns, five reindeer skins, one bear's skin, ten bushels of feathers, a cloak of bear's or otter's skin, two ship-ropes (each sixty ells long), one made of whale's and the other of seal's skin.

"Ohthere moreover said that the land of the Northmen was very long and very narrow; all that is fit either for pasture or ploughing lies along the sea coast, which, however, is in some parts very cloddy; along the eastern side are wild moors, extending a long way up parallel to the cultivated land. The Finlanders inhabit these moors, and the cultivated land is broadest to the eastward; and, altogether, the more northward it lies, the more narrow it is. Eastward it may perhaps be sixty miles broad, in some places broader; about the middle, thirty miles, or somewhat more; and northward, Ohthere says (where it is narrowest), it may be only three miles across from the sea to the moors, which, however, are in some parts so wide, that a man could scarcely pass over them in two weeks, though in other parts perhaps in six days. Then parallel with this land southward is Sweoland, on the other side of the moors, extending quite to the northward; and running even with the northern part of it is Cwenaland. The Cwenas sometimes make incursions against the Northmen over these moors, and sometimes the Northmen on them; there are very large meres of fresh water beyond the moors, and the Cwenas carry their ships overland into the meres, whence they make depredations on the Northmen; they have ships that are very small and very light.

"Ohthere said that the shire which he inhabited is called Halgoland. He says that no human being abode in any fixed habitation to the north of him. There is a port to the south of this land, which is called Sciringes-heal. Thither he said that a man could not sail in a month, if he watched in the night, and every day had a fair wind;

and all the while he shall sail along the coast; and on his right hand first is Island, and then the islands which are between Island and this land. Then this land continues quite to Sciringes-heal; and all the way on the left is Norway. To the south of Sciringes- heal a great sea runs up a vast way into the country, and is so wide that no man can see across it. (Jutland is opposite on the other side, and then Sealand.) This sea lies many hundred miles up into the land. Ohthere further says that he sailed in five days from Sciringes-heal to that port which men call AEt-Haethum, which stands between the Winedae, the Saxons, and the Angles, and is subject to the Danes.

"When Ohthere sailed to this place from Sciringes-heal, Denmark was on his left, and on his right the wide sea, for three days; and for the two days before he came to Haethum, on his right hand was Jutland, Sealand, and many islands; all which lands were inhabited by the English, before they came hither; and for these two days the islands which are subject to Denmark were on his left."

"Wulfstan said that he went from Haethum to Truso in seven days and nights, and that the ship was running under sail all the way. Weonodland was on his right, and Langland, Laeland, Falster, and Sconey, on his left, all which land is subject to Denmark. "Then on our left we had the land of the Burgundians, who have a king to themselves. Then, after the land of the Burgundians, we had on our left the lands that have been called from the earliest times Ble-kingey, and Meore, and Eowland, and Gotland, all which territory is subject to the Sweons; and Weonodland was all the way on our right, as far as Weissel-mouth. The Weissel is a very large river, and near it lie Witland and Weonodland. Witland belongs to the people of Eastland; and out of Weonodland flows the river Weissel, which empties itself afterwards into Estmere. This lake, called Estmere, is about fifteen miles broad. Then runs the Ilfing east (of the Weissel) into Estmere, from that lake on the banks of which stands Truso. These two rivers come out together into Estmere, the Ilfing east from Eastland, and the Weissel south from Weonodland. Then the Weissel deprives the Ilfing of its name, and, flowing from the west part of the lake, at length empties itself northward into the sea, whence this point is called the Weissel-mouth. This country called Eastland is very extensive, and there are in it many towns, and in every town is a king. There is a great quantity of honey and fish; and even the king and the richest men drink mare's milk, whilst the poor and the slaves drink mead. There is a vast deal of war and contention amongst the different tribes of this nation. There is no ale brewed amongst the Estonians, but they have mead in profusion.

"There is also this custom with the Estonians, that when anyone dies the corpse continues unburnt with the relations and friends for at least a month, sometimes two; and the bodies of kings and illustrious men, according to their respective wealth, lie sometimes even for half a year before the corpse is burned, and the body continues above ground in the house, during which time drinking and sports are prolonged till the day on which the body is consumed. Then, when it is carried to the funeral pile, the substance of the deceased, which remains after these drinking festivities and sports, is divided into five or six heaps; sometimes into more, according to the proportion of what he happens to be worth. These heaps are so disposed that the largest heap shall be about one mile from the town; and so gradually the smaller at lesser intervals, till all the wealth is divided, so that the least heap shall be nearest the town where the corpse lies.

"Then all those are to be summoned together who have the fleetest horses in the land, for a wager of skill, within the distance of five or six miles from these heaps; and they all ride a race toward the substance of the deceased. Then comes the man that has the winning horse toward the first and largest heap, and so each after other, till the whole is seized upon. He procures, however, the least heap who takes that which is nearest the town; and then everyone rides away with his share, and keeps the whole of it. On account of this custom fleet horses in that country are wonderfully dear. When the wealth of the deceased has been thus exhausted, then they carry out his corpse from the house and burn it, together with his weapons and clothes; and generally they spend his whole substance by the long continuance of the body within the house, together with what they lay in heaps along the road, which the strangers run for, and take away.

"It is also an established custom with the Estonians that the dead bodies of every tribe or family shall be burned, and if any man findeth a single bone unconsumed, they shall be fined to a considerable amount. These Estonians also have the power of producing artificial cold; and it is thus the dead body continues so long above ground without putrefying, on which they produce this artificial cold; and, though a man should set two vessels full of ale or of water, they contrive that either shall be completely frozen over; and this equally the same in the summer as in the winter."

Now will we speak about those parts of Europe that lie to the south of the river Danube; and first of all, concerning Greece. The sea which flows along the eastern side of Constantinople (a Grecian city) is called Propontis. To the north of this Grecian city an arm of the sea shoots up westward from the Euxine; and to the west by north the mouths of the river Danube empty themselves south-east into the Euxine. To the south and west of these mouths are the Moessians, a tribe of Greeks; to the west of the city are the Thracians; and to the west also are the Macedonians. To the south of this city, towards the southern part of that arm of the sea which is called the Egean, Athens and Corinth are situated. And to the west by south of Corinth is the land of Achaia, near the Mediterranean. To the west of Achaia, along the Mediterranean, is Dalmatia, on the north side of the sea; to the north of Dalmatia are the boundaries of Bulgaria and Istria. To the south of Istria is that part of the Mediterranean which is called the Adriatic; to the west are the Alps; and to the north that desert which is between the Carinthians and the Bulgarians.

Italy, which is of great length west by north, and also east by south, is surrounded by the Mediterranean on every side but towards the west-north. At that end of it lie the Alps, which begin westward from the Mediterranean, in the Narbonense country, and end eastward in Dalmatia, near the [Adriatic] sea.

With respect to the territory called Gallia Belgica, to the east of it is the river Rine, to the south the Alps, to the west by south the sea called the British Ocean, and to the north, on the other side of the arm of the ocean, is Britannia. The land to the west of the river Loire is AEquitania; to the south of AEquitania is some part of the Narbonense; to the west by south is the territory of Spain; and to the south the ocean. To the south of the Narbonense is the Mediterranean, where the Rone empties itself into the sea, having Provence both on the east and west. Over the Pyrenean wastes is Ispania citerior, to the west of which, by north, is AEquitania, and the province of Gascony to the north. Provence has to the north of it the Alps; to the south of it is the Mediterranean; to the north-east of it are the Burgundians; and the people of Gascony to the west.

Spain is triangular, and entirely guarded on the outside by the sea, either by the great ocean or by the Mediterranean, and also well guarded within over the land. One of the angles lies south-west against the island of Gades, the second eastward against the Narbonense territory, and the third north-west against Braganza, a town of Gallicia. And against Scotland (i.e., Ireland), over the arm of the sea, in a straight line with the mouth of the Shannon, is Ispania ulterior. To the west of it is the ocean; and to the south and east of it, northward of the Mediterranean, is Ispania citerior; to the north of which are the lands of Equitania; to the north-east is the weald of the Pyrenees, to the east the Narbonense, and to the south the Mediterranean.

With regard to the island Britannia, it is of considerable length to the north-east, being eight hundred miles long and only two hundred miles broad. To the south of it, on the other side of the arm of the sea, is Gallia Belgica; to the west, on the other side of an arm of the sea, is the island Ibernia, and to the northward the Orkney Isles. Igbernia, which we call Scotland, is surrounded on every side with the ocean; and hence, because the rays of the setting sun strike on it with less interruption than on other countries, the weather is milder there than it is in Britain. Thence, to the west- north of Ibernia, is that utmost land called Thila, which is known to a few men only, on account of its exceeding great distance.

Thus have we now sufficiently described all the landmarks of Europe, according to their respective situations.

ELEGIAC VERSES BY WILLIAM WORDSWORTH

In Memory of a Brother Drowned at Sea.

TO THE DAISY.

Sweet Flower! belike one day to have
A place upon thy poet's grave,
I welcome thee once more:
But He, who was on land, at sea,
My Brother, too, in loving thee,
Although he loved more silently,
Sleeps by his native shore.

Ah! hopeful, hopeful was the day
When to that ship he bent his way,
To govern and to guide:
His wish was gained: a little time
Would bring him back in manhood's prime
And free for life, these hills to climb;
With all his wants supplied.

And full of hope day followed day
While that stout Ship at anchor lay
Beside the shores of Wight;
The May had then made all things green;
And, floating there, in pomp serene,
That Ship was goodly to be seen,
His pride and his delight!

Yet then, when called ashore, he sought
The tender peace of rural thought:
In more than happy mood
To your abodes, bright daisy Flowers!
He then would steal at leisure hours,
And loved you glittering in your bowers,
A starry multitude.

But hark the word!—the ship is gone; -
Returns from her long course:- anon
Sets sail:- in season due,
Once more on English earth they stand:
But, when a third time from the land
They parted, sorrow was at hand
For Him and for his crew.

Ill-fated Vessel?—ghastly shock!
- At length delivered from the rock,
The deep she hath regained;
And through the stormy night they steer;
Labouring for life, in hope and fear,
To reach a safer shore—how near,
Yet not to be attained!

"Silence!" the brave Commander cried;
To that calm word a shriek replied,
It was the last death-shriek.
- A few (my soul oft sees that sight)
Survive upon the tall mast's height;
But one dear remnant of the night -
For Him in vain I seek.

Six weeks beneath the moving sea
He lay in slumber quietly;
Unforced by wind or wave
To quit the Ship for which he died,
(All claims of duty satisfied);
And there they found him at her side;
And bore him to the grave.

Vain service! yet not vainly done
For this, if other end were none,
That He, who had been cast
Upon a way of life unmeet
For such a gentle Soul and sweet,
Should find an undisturbed retreat
Near what he loved, at last -

That neighbourhood of grove and field
To Him a resting-place should yield,
A meek man and a brave!
The birds shall sing and ocean make
A mournful murmur for HIS sake;
And Thou, sweet Flower, shalt sleep and wake
Upon his senseless grave.